Belfast Studies in Language, Culture and Politics

General Editors
John M. Kirk and Dónall P. Ó Baoill

Other volumes under consideration

www.bslcp.com

Queen's University
Belfast

Language and Politics
Northern Ireland, the Republic of Ireland, and Scotland

Edited by

John M. Kirk and Dónall P. Ó Baoill

Cló Ollscoil na Banríona
Belfast 2000

First published in 2000
Cló Ollscoil na Banríona
Queen's University Belfast
Belfast, BT7 1NN

Belfast Studies in Language, Culture and Politics
www.bslcp.com

This book has received support from the Cultural Diversity Programme of the
Community Relations Council, which aims to encourage acceptance and
understanding of cultural diversity, *Foras na Gaeilge* and *Tha Boord o Ulstèr-Scotch*. The views expressed do not necessarily reflect those of the NI
Community Relations Council, *Foras na Gaeilge* or *Tha Boord o Ulstèr-Scotch*.

British Library Cataloguing-in-Publication Data
A catalogue record for this book is available from the British Library.

ISBN 0 85389 791 3

Typeset in Times New Roman 10

Printed by Textflow, Belfast

The papers in this volume were presented at
Language, Politics and Ethnolinguistics
a Symposium on Language and Politics
held on 12 August 2000
and at
Dialect2000: Language Links
an International Conference
on the Languages of Scotland and Ireland
9-16 August 2000
Queen's University Belfast
an event of the Irish-Scottish Academic Initiative

CONTENTS

Contributors

Mark Adair, a graduate in Modern History from Queen's University Belfast, is currently Director of the European Programme of the Northern Ireland Community Relations Council.

Dr. Alasdair J. Allan gained his PhD from the University of Aberdeen in 1998 for a thesis entitled *New Founs fae Auld Larachs: Leid-Plannin for Scots*. He is currently Parliamentary Assistant to Michael Russell, SNP Shadow Minister for Culture, Broadcasting and Gaelic in the Scottish Parliament.

Dr. Liam S. Andrews is free-lance translator living in Belfast. His Queen's University Belfast PhD thesis, for which he graduated in 2000, is entitled *Unionism and Nationalism and the Irish Language 1893-1933*.

Dr. Robert J. Cormack is Pro-Vice-Chancellor for Learning and Teaching and Professor of Sociology at Queen's University Belfast.

Dr. Seán Farren is a Member of the Northern Ireland Executive and Minister for Higher and Further Education, Training and Employment. Previously, he was a Senior Lecturer in Education at the University of Ulster at Coleraine.

Dr. Mari FitzDuff is Professor of Conflict Studies and Director of the Initiative on Conflict Resolution and Ethnicity (INCORE) between the University of Ulster at Magee College, Derry/Londonderry and United Nations University. Previously, she was Director of the Northern Ireland Community Relations Council.

Nadette Foley is Chief Officer of the Multi-Cultural Resource Centre (N.I.) in Belfast. Previously, she was the Director of the Irish Refugee Council in Dublin, and she has also worked in Pakistan with refugees from Afghanistan.

Dr. Manfred Görlach is Professor of English Linguistics and Medieval Studies at the University of Cologne. His latest book, *18th-Century English*, is published in December 2000. The next will be *A History of Scots*, co-authored with Dr. Katja Lenz, in 2001, both published by Carl Winter Universitätsverlag, Heidelberg.

Tom Hadden is Professor of Law at the Centre for International and Comparative Human Rights Law, Queen's University Belfast, a Commissioner of the Northern Ireland Human Rights Commission, and founder of *Fortnight* magazine.

Dr. Dauvit Horsbroch is a Teaching Assistant in the Department of Celtic at the University of Aberdeen and a prominent Scots-language activist. With Steve Murdoch, he has authored two Aiberdeen Univairsitie Scots Leid Quorum discussion documents entitled *Daena Haud yer Wheisht, Haud Yer Ain!* (1996) and *Kennin yer Earse fae yer Alba: The Scottish Office, the Gaelic Lobby and the Scots Language* (1998), produced in Scots and in English.

Dr. John M. Kirk is a Lecturer in English at Queen's University Belfast. His University of Sheffield PhD thesis is entitled *Aspects of the Grammar in a Corpus of Dramatic Texts in Scots*.

P. A. MagLochlainn was a Grammar School Teacher of French, Irish and Latin before taking early retirement on health grounds. He is currently President of the Northern Ireland Gay Rights Association.

Helen Ó Murchú is a Founder Member and past President of the European Bureau for Lesser Used Languages and is currently Director/Stiúrthóir of *Comhar ma Múinteoirí Gaeilge* which is concerned with Irish-medium education. Her publications include *The Irish Language* (1985) and *Irish: Facing the Future* (1999).

Bob McCullough is the writer of the weekly *Deaf Talkabout* column in the *Belfast Telegraph*, for which he was presented a citation for spreading deaf awareness from the British Deaf Association during its Congress in Belfast in August 2000.

Dr. Dónall P. Ó Baoill is Professor of Irish at Queen's University Belfast.

Dónall Ó Riagáin is Special Adviser to the European Bureau for Lesser Used Languages and formerly served both as President and Secretary General of that organisation. He also works as an independent consultant.

Ian J. Parsley is a Director at the Ulster-Scots Academy and a free-lance language consultant who runs the electronic discussion list *Ullans-L*.

Anna Man-Wah Watson is Director of the Chinese Welfare Association (N.I.), Belfast.

Acknowledgements

We wish to acknowledge the help and support which they have received with the preparation of this volume from Vivien Dodds, Patrick McWilliams, Trevor Meighan, Kay Muhr, Colin Neilands and Ian Parsley. For their financial support, we are grateful to the Cultural Diversity Program of the Community Relations Council and to *Foras na Gaeilge* and *Tha Boord o Ulstèr-Scotch*.

We are also deeply grateful to all the contributors to the volume, for both participating in the Symposium and the Conference and for allowing us to publish their presentations. Although the symposium discussions after each set of presentations were extremely stimulating in the cross-fertlisation of information and experience from the Irish-language and Scots-language movements and many notable and memorable contributions were made, including those by Alasdair Allan, Marace Dareau, Sheila Douglas, Robin Glendinning, Manfred Görlach, Dauvit Horsbroch, Aodán Mac Póilin, Derrick McClure, Helen Ó Murchú, Dónall Ó Riagáin, and many others, we regret that it has not proved possible to include transcripts in this volume. We are also grateful to Pat McAlister, Director of the Linguistic Diversity Branch within the Department of Culture, Arts and Leisure, and to Mark Adair for their willingness to act as symposium rapporteurs. Finally, but by no means least, in connection with the Symposium, we are especially grateful to Noel Thompson for his most professional chairmanship, to Jim McCloskey for operating the sound system, and to Colin Neilands for so nimbly fielding the roving microphone.

We are also grateful for the institutional support which they have received from Queen's University Belfast and in particular from the School of English and Dr. Ellen Douglas-Cowie, Head of School.

John M. Kirk and Dónall P. Ó Baoill
Belfast, November 2000

Preface: Kosovo in the Spring

R J Cormack

KFOR tanks and armoured vehicles surround the airport in Prishtina and provide an ominous welcome to Kosovo. The trip from the airport into the city provides some evidence of war damage but also of recent and ongoing reconstruction. The Prishtina Grand Hotel is anything but grand. Water and electricity supply is intermittent, although improving month by month.

Sitting on the dilapidated hotel terrace, the first and foremost impression is of the number and diversity of NGOs operating in Kosovo (estimates vary between two and three hundred). The modern versions of Second World War Jeeps, now in bright colours, slowly parade down the main street displaying their various logos: Red Cross, Red Crescent, Oxfam, Caribinieri, Body Shop, Los Angeles Police Department (on bikes), Save the Children and so on. The local economy is being seriously distorted by the presence of these groups and their staff especially given the very low incomes of Kosovars. A clear exit strategy will be necessary in order not to leave a gaping hole in the economy.

The University of Prishtina is celebrating its thirtieth anniversary. It is a hopeful moment after a sad history in recent years. At its inception, the subjects of the University were taught in Serbian and Albanian. The Albanians document a history of Serbian attempts to exclude them from the University both as staff and as students. Albanian students demonstrated against Serbian exclusionary tactics in 1981. The few thousand students in 1981 grew to hundreds of thousands of fellow Albanians in the demonstrations in 1988 and 1989 against the increasing 'Serbianisation' of Kosovo.

Predictably, both sides fear the other. The Albanians fear the creation of a Greater Serbia; while the Serbians fear a Greater Albania. Every aspect of life appears to be contested. 'Kosova' is the Albanian form, while 'Kosovo' is the Serbian form. Towns have alternative Serbian and Albanian spellings. Squeezed in between these two major ethnic groups are smaller groupings of Turks, Roma (Gypsies), Montenegrins and Croats. The Serbs are nominally Orthodox while the Albanians are nominally Muslim. Denis Murray, the BBC's Ireland Correspondent, was sent to Kosovo to make a film reflecting on the connections to Northern Ireland. He comments: '...as I told Kosovar and Serb alike, I had an instant FEEL for the place. Who from Northern Ireland wouldn't.'[1]

In the summer of 1981, the University was entirely under Serbian control and was transformed into a Serbian language institution. Albanian academics set up a parallel institution operating in kitchens and cellars throughout Prishtina. Following the NATO intervention in the Spring of 1999, the Albanians reclaimed the University of Prishtina and, to all extent and purposes, expelled all remaining Serb academics. Tim Judah[2] reports that three Serbs were executed at the University in June 1999. Ten months later, when I asked the newly elected student leaders about this incident, none knew anything of this revenge attack.

The United Nations Mission in Kosovo (UNMIK) administration has announced its intention of renaming the *University of Prishtina* as the *University of Kosovo/a* to try to emphasise its inclusive and all-Kosovo character. UNMIK has appointed an International Administrator for the University: Professor Michael Daxner, formerly Rector of the University of Oldenburg in Germany. Professor Daxner is running the University alongside the Albanian Rector, Professor Kelmendi. The Serbs challenge the legitimacy of the current arrangements and have no involvement in the University apart from the remnants of provision located in Mitrovica (mainly a mining school), one of the very few areas of Kosovo where there remains a significant number of Serbs.

UNMIK, with World Bank funding, has commissioned the Council of Europe to provide assistance and advice on restructuring the University. Primarily the University requires a new law within which to operate and a new set of statutes governing the internal arrangements for its work. I have been invited to join a team of three on this project.

The similarities to Northern Ireland, Denis Murray observed, are marked. However, while our divisions are deep and of long-standing, we do not face the future as a zero sum game between the two communities, or not, at least, if our politicians sign up to the Belfast Agreement. The Serbs almost succeeded in 'ethnically cleansing' Kosovo of Albanian Kosovars before the NATO intervention. To nearly every observer's surprise, these Kosovars returned in large numbers. Kosovo was part of a relatively successful state, Tito's Yugoslavia; while Hoxha's Albania was a desperate failure and hence held few attractions for Albanian Kosovars who sought refuge from Serbian atrocities. Revenge has since been taken by returning Albanian Kosovars and present-day Kosovo has very few Serbs left.

The hatred between Albanian and Serbian in Kosovo is palpable. The hatreds in Northern Ireland are no less real although perhaps not as widespread throughout the two communities. The distinguished Queen's historian, A.T.Q. Stewart once said: 'There is an almost visceral hatred between the two communities. People in Kosovo lived together for years - then someone made a mistake. We have a mild form of that here.'[3] What kept us hovering on the brink of a Kosovo, without ever falling over into all-out war, is a matter for much contentious debate involving, for example, arguments for the restraining role of the paramilitaries, and of civil society and its institutions; the mediating effect of women's groups; the Army and Police as buffers; and policy interventions such as fair employment legislation. The scenes of destruction and the uncertain future for both Albanians and Serbs are reminders to us of how close we came to the awfulness that is contemporary Kosovo.

Notes

[1]   Denis Murray, *Belfast Telegraph*, 12.5.00

[2]   Tim Judah, *Kosovo*, (London: Yale University Press, 2000).

[3]   Quoted in Susan McKay, *Northern Protestants: An Unsettled People* (Belfast: Blackstaff Press, 2000)

Introduction: Language, Politics and English

John M Kirk and Dónall P Ó Baoill

Symposium on 12 August 2000

This book arises directly from the Symposium on *Language, Politics and Ethnolinguistics* which we organised, and which was held on 12 August 2000 at Queen's University Belfast as part of *Dialect2000: Language Links*, an International Conference on the Languages of Scotland and Ireland, at which some of the larger papers in the volume were originally presented.

The Symposium was timely. The Belfast Good Friday Agreement of 1998 had recognised the central importance of Language in Northern Ireland by creating for it one of the six North-South Implementation Bodies[1]. By the same stroke, the Agreement had recognised the commonality of the Language agenda with the Republic of Ireland: what was to happen in each jurisdiction would now come to affect the other (as Dauvit Horsbroch shows in this volume). By the time of the Symposium, the North-South Body had split itself into two cross-border agencies: *Foras na Gaeilge* for Irish and *Tha Boord o Ulstèr-Scotch* for Ulster Scots, each of which were busily drafting their corporate plans. Within the Northern Ireland Executive, responsibility for Language had fallen to the Department of Culture, Arts and Leisure, which had in turn established a Linguistic Diversity Branch. Its remit was extended to the province's 'ethnic minority' or 'non-indigenous' or 'lesser used' or 'regional and minority' languages. The Branch, too, was busily identifying its role and function and drawing up appropriate strategies. With all these accomplishments, the Language lobby must have felt proud at the considerable progress which had been made.

A second significant element of the Good Friday Agreement was its undertaking to prepare a Bill of Rights for Northern Ireland. So central to the political progress had Language become that, by the Symposium, the draft proposal had come to contain provision for the protection of language use; besides, it had become clear that it was not uncommon in other parts of the world for language rights and human rights to go hand-in-hand, as Mari FitzDuff shows in her paper.

A third progressive element of the Agreement is its Equality Agenda which proscribes discrimination on the nine grounds of religion, political opinion, gender, race, disability, age, marital status, dependants and sexual orientation, already incorporated in Section 75 of the Northern Ireland Act, 1998. For gay people and deaf people, communication and language use is at the core of discrimination against them.

First and foremost, however, this volume of papers is about the linguistic diversity of Northern Ireland. Linguistic diversity is much wider than Irish and Ulster-Scots, although so far they have received the greatest attention.

At this unprecedented junction in the history of language in Northern Ireland, when considerable planning was underway, we felt that it was timely to take a critical look at what was happening. We had several immediate goals, as realised in this volume:

(i)   *To look at the entirety of the linguistic situation in Northern Ireland*
(ii)   *To look at comparisons in other parts of the world*
(iii)   *To document the present legislative situation and its evolution*
(iv)   *To reflect more abstractly about the local situation*
(v)   *To examine the similarities and differences in Scotland, especially with regard to Scots*

This volume offers a set of papers which document the history and background to the linguistic situation especially in Northern Ireland and the present legislative measures.

Dónall Ó Riagáin shows that the present arrangements in the Belfast/Good Friday Agreement and the proposed Bill of Rights originated some fifty years ago in the UN's Universal Declaration of Human Rights of 1948. He traces the steady progress in Europe which culminated in the *European Charter for Regional and Minority Languages*, upon which the Belfast/Good Friday Agreement is predicated, and which the UK Government (but alas not the Republic of Ireland Government) has signed. We are pleased to be able to publish such a well-documented account of this steady evolution, for which Dónall, as the long-serving Secretary General of the European Bureau for Lesser Used Languages, can take considerable credit.

Seán Farren presents an overview of the institutional infrastructure in Northern Ireland following the Good Friday Agreement, or 'manifesto', as he calls it. He considers it an exciting challenge to move from an acceptance of the Belfast/Good Friday Agreement to making available space and resources to enable recognition and appreciation of the linguistic as well as cultural diversity of Northern Ireland. It is good to have ministerial reassurance that, with respect to the *European Charter*, steering and working groups have been set up to decide how it should be implemented for Northern Ireland.

Tom Hadden reproduces the discussion document prepared by the Northern Ireland Human Rights Council on possible guarantees for language rights in a new Northern Ireland Bill of Rights as part of its consultation process.

This volume also provides a critical comparison between the linguistic situation in Northern Ireland and that in Scotland both with regard to Irish and Scottish Gaelic and to Scots and Ulster Scots.

Dauvit Horsbroch and **Alasdair Allen** give separate responses to the evolving legislative and government-institutional arrangements in both jurisdictions from a Scottish perspective, where Gaelic has traditionally done better than Scots.

Dauvit Horsbroch writes *in masterful written Scots*, which would probably not be too dissimilar to any emerging standardised form of the language, and certainly a model for revivalists in Ulster to consider. Among his many points of comparison are:

- that, whereas the situation for Scots in Scotland has improved as a result of the advent of the Scottish Parliament and of more general cultural changes , Scots in Ulster, has fared better and differently. He recognises not only that language planners in Ulster now have a unprecedented freedom to build up Scots, but that, with fewer speakers, less literature, and less knowledge generally, they have an ever greater freedom than in Scotland where a larger and more knowledgeable population will exercise more control and where for many the Scots language is regarded as no more than 'an element of everyday speech', i.e. of everyday English.

- that the double irony whereby Scots has been adopted as part of the identity of Protestant Ulster Unionism, not only to match Irish as a symbol of Catholic Ulster Nationalism, but also to serve as a retentionist badge of the common British identity. In Scotland, the more the promotion of Scots is adopted by the Scottish National Party, the more it will come to be viewed as a separatist badge of Scottish independence.

- that Scots in Ulster is taken far more seriously by the devolved Government and might well leap considerably further forward in the near future, well ahead of the small recent gains in Scotland.

- that Scots in Ulster is considerably better funded than in Scotland. Even in the Republic of Ireland, more funding is given to Scots in Ulster than the Scottish office has ever given to it in its home country.

To move Scots on from here, Horsbroch urges people on both sides of the *sheuch* to get together and to start speaking Scots to each other as the one language, but to *caw canny* on the writing of it down and to avoid any outlandishness.

This volume presents three authoritative and scholarly papers on the background to Irish and Ulster Scots.

We are especially pleased to reproduce **Liam Andrews's** historical account of the Irish Language revivalist movement from the seventeenth-century plantation to present-day West Belfast. Liam takes a fresh, critical look at the Society for the Preservation of Irish, the Gaelic Athletic Association, and the Gaelic League; by the early twentieth century, he identifies two main driving forces behind revival:

'Catholic Communalism' and 'Irish-Language Communalism', each of which has striven for dominance.

We are honoured to reproduce **Manfred Görlach's** plenary lecture entitled: 'Ulster Scots: A Language?' because he universalises the linguistic situation of Ulster Scots/Ullans by recognising that 'languageness' is usually a matter of degree, defined by diagnostic criteria such as *abstand, ausbau, attitude,* and *acquisition,* or such as *standardisation, autonomy, historicity* and *vitality.* At the same time, historically, languages erode or become revitalised, further processes the degrees of which may again be judged against Görlach's own criteria, which he sets out explicitly. He proposes the useful distinction of restricting 'Ulster Scots' to refer to the vestigial dialect of Scots still spoken in the province, and 'Ullans' to the new written dialect, which is described in a separate paper by **John Kirk**. Görlach is sceptical that there will be support behind revival even among people who 'love their dialect' as it is and suggests that for many people accent alone is a sufficient marker of group or ethnic identity.

Görlach concludes with the strictly *linguistic* definition of revival Ulster Scots as 'a second dialect relearnt to stress ethnicity' [*presumably* Ulster-Scottishness]. This 'second dialect', he elaborates, is 'largely parasitical since competence in it largely depends on the prior acquisition of another language of wider communication, English ... [it is] an enriched variety'. These are definitions are borrowed from a study of Pitcairnese on Norfolk Island, where they are used to define the notion of a *cant.*[1] It is not unusual for unique situations to require unique concepts. This fresh categorisation adds to three others previously identified by John Kirk,[2] who discusses how Ulster Scots (or Scots in general) may be categorised as:

- a *half-language* or *semi-language* because Scots no longer has the status of a full language which it once had, its functions having become restricted.

- an *apperceptional language* because it is cognitively categorised as a language by its supporters, who vehemently believe its categorisation, although its linguistic independence as a language cannot be demonstrated.

- a *kin language* in that its formal relationship with and subordination to the dominant standard language of English has denied it its due recognition and rights.

In view of the provision for Language in the Bill of Rights, it has become more important than ever for the nature of the present spoken reality of all languages in Northern Ireland to be clearly identified and defined, for *linguistic* definitions to be separated from *political* definitions and in turn from political *recognitions,* and for the status of *speech* to be sharply contrasted with experiments in *written prose.*

Against this background of Irish and Ulster Scots, this volume extends the debate to include all aspects of linguistic diversity. We are mindful that the present institutional and legislative arrangements came about as a result of political lobbying and agitation, of which a major plank was discrimination, a denial of linguistic rights, a lack of equality. Many Irish-speakers and Irish-enthusiasts wish for the affairs of their life to be conducted in Irish and for their children to be educated in Irish: why ever not? And so for some Ulster Scots enthusiasts, the arguments are in their fullest form the same. The arguments of the ethnic minority communities are of a different order and very directly involve those communities' use of English as well as their own languages.

Consider our constituencies from which we sought representation at the Symposium and in turn in this volume[3]:

- The **deaf community** suffers from a regular and widespread inability to communicate within English at will with the non-deaf community. This discrimination also needs political accommodation. It is a real problem and it visibly and physically exists.
- **Women**[4] have suffered real grievances from the way English continues to exclude them by its sexist and gender-bound reference system. This regular and widespread discrimination and expressed exclusion needs political accommodation.
- **Speakers of non-indigenous or ethnic minority or lesser used languages** as well as members of the travelling community can have difficulties with the quality of their English, with literacy in general, and with the status and standing in Northern Ireland of their own language. Second-language education in fluency in spoken English and in literacy in written English needs political accommodation. The future status and role (if any) of these languages need consideration.
- Like any subgroup, **gays and lesbians**[5] add to the rich variety of expressiveness in English; but their way of using English is no argument for homophobia or discrimination especially in the workplace or in any group or organisation supported or funded by public or statutory bodies governed by Section 75 of the Northern Ireland Act 1998. Their agenda, too, with an active constituency of some 10% of the population, needs political accommodation.

At the core of this volume are a set of six invited presentations by activists and community spokespersons in response to two central questions which we had set each of them in advance:

- *Are members of your community (or do they feel) discriminated against on linguistic grounds? Is the discrimination real or perceived?*

- *What expectations do members of your community have of the implementation of the Good Friday agreement, with its provision of*

Language Bodies and its strong Bill of Human Rights, with regard to an improvement of the situation and political accommodation?

A strength of the Symposium – now reflected in these papers – was its demonstration of very real support and solidarity between and for all these groups and a very real sense of optimism for change for the better through current political and legislative measures. There is overwhelming agreement – shared among Irish–language and Ulster-Scots activists, too – that all aspects of linguistic diversity need to be accommodated through the same measures, and that no one group should be awarded beyond its due or shout.

Bob McCulloch presents the genuine difficulties which Northern Ireland's 4,000 strong deaf community encounter in interacting with their hearing peers in English, in performing in the education system, and in being included in the decision-making process about themselves. There is very real discrimination, but through the Bill of Human Rights the deaf community is looking for empowerment and equality and above all in inclusion in the decision-making process.

Anna Man-Wah Watson presents the numerous problems which Northern Ireland's **8,000 strong Cantonese speakers** in Northern Ireland encounter in everyday interaction, in education, and in health care, social work, and other support encounters when they speak no or very little English and when there is almost no public information in Cantonese. For many, their only source of support is at home, but often that is not the support the individual needs.

Nadette Foley presents the similar problems which the (often illiterate) **speakers of as many as 50 lesser used languages** in Northern Ireland. She welcomes the discussion around current legislative innovations as she considers it essential for Northern Ireland to move forward from a 'both communities'/'two traditions' agenda to a recognition that Northern Ireland has become a multi-cultural society. For speakers of lesser used languages, it is a matter of having the rights to engage with the statutory system in your mother tongue, as well as of wishing to strengthen and maintain your cultural identity. \

P.A. MagLochlainn addresses the difficulties which the **gay speakers** can face when hurt through linguistic misuse directed at their identity. He feels that verbal abuse may well contribute to gay suicides. Current equality legislation will help to protect gay people and to bring anti-gay discrimination out into the open.

Helen Ó Murchú[6] presents the case of discrimination against **speakers of Irish** (at least 140,000 persons indicating some knowledge of it, passive or active, in Northern Ireland) from considerable experience and conviction as one of the most successful campaigners for rights for Irish speakers. She urges that legislation is insufficient to protect or ensure language or human rights unless effective forms of implementation and monitoring of results are clearly built in. Finally, she offers some critical challenges to the *An Foras Teanga* that its role and practices over the development of public policy.

Ian Parsley, a linguist, not an activist[7], in a remarkable *tour de force* in Ulster Scots, asserts the case of discrimination against **speakers of Ulster Scots** in broadcasting, in the Civil Service, and in education, where hardly any Ulster Scots language or Ulster Scots culture is taught. He welcomes the *European Charter* and the Cross-border Language Bodies as the most important developments in the last 400 years. At the same time, he acknowledges that people are reluctant to use Ulster Scots in public, and that it is hard to identify the 'Ulster-Scots speaking community', to which legislation usually refers.

This volume also transcends the local situation especially with regard to Irish and Ulster Scots by universalising it through abstract and theoretical reflections, and numerous international comparisons, too numerous to detail here, except to draw attention to those in Mari FitzDuff's and Manfred Görlach's papers.

Mari FitzDuff universalises the linguistic situation in Northern Ireland by considering language not to be a cause of conflict but a tool with which you sort out other conflict issues. She suggests that the widespread competition between languages is usually about competition for power, respect, belonging and validation. With reference to South Africa, she doubts whether the existence of legal safeguards or strong safeguards on equality or human rights are sufficient to prevent people from using or misusing language when they want to assert and divide.

Mark Adair urges us all to think in terms across leaking categorical boundaries and mongrelisation in order to face up to the prospect of Northern Ireland as a pluralist society, and of the creation of a socially inclusive and cohesive society, with proper citizenship, from out of all of the difference around us.

He acknowledges that the borders between our cultural and political experiences are real but also recognises that they are no longer pure for they also overlap. He urges everyone to make diversity work, as the papers in this volume implicitly urge, and cautions against mono-culturalism.

Although the papers are inevitably on individual aspects of linguistic diversity, the thrust of their accumulation is a recognition of the legitimacy of each and every one of them.

Which languages? Which communities?

Tempting though it might seem, it is not straightforward to think of 'speakers of a language' forming a 'community' or even the 'community of that language'. There are many activists and sympathisers who don't speak the particular language. There are others who belong to two communities – especially if they speak Irish as well as Ulster Scots. There are many who feel that such 'communities' are defined by wider issues of 'culture' and 'identity' of which 'the language' is only a part. Ian Parsley wonders whether there is a community of 'Ulster Scots speakers' and, even if there were, who would represent them. Whereas those Language constituencies identified in the Belfast Good Friday Agreement have done well, we feel that neither all 'languages' or 'constituencies' have been represented. We are eager to help those others to let their voice be heard. We would naturally support Anna Watson's plea that the inclusion of the languages of the local ethnic minorities should not be as an after-thought.

We welcome the idea of a Linguistic Diversity Branch established on grounds of discrimination and the imperative of redress and non-discriminatory practice, and equality. Our difficulty with the idea is that it doesn't go far enough, and that that it excludes the major element of diversity and the major agent of discrimination: *English*, and it is a whopping gap. English is, for many, both the source and the vehicle of discrimination as well as being the language of their community. The entrenched polarities between 'Irish' and 'Ulster-Scots', and between the 'Irish-speaking community' and the 'Ulster-Scots-speaking community' are becoming revised into fresh polarities between the 'both of them' and 'English', or both of them' and 'the rest of us'. As Mark Adair argues, most people are mongrels who are not water-tight in any one community.

The unprecedented support for Irish has come from political decisions in response to arguments about discrimination, as Helen Ó Murchú argues so persuasively. Yet all our other constituencies (the 'deaf community', the 'blind community', the 'ethnic minority communities', the 'gay and lesbian community', all already protected by recent equality legislation) and also others unable to accept our invitations to participate (e.g. the 'women's community', the 'travelling community') also claim discrimination through English. That is why we feel justified in urging that the argument of discrimination, used so favourably for support for the Irish- and Scots-speaking communities, needs to be used again in favour of English-speaking communities. Whereas the Linguistic Diversity Agenda has been extended to Cantonese and Urdu and potentially other ethnic minority languages, it now also needs to be extended to include *English*.

Ethnolinguistics

None of the present papers address the question of ethnolinguistics and the emerging fact that, throughout Northern Ireland, without direction or guidance, without Academy or Agency, Catholics and Protestants are beginning to diverge in their speech habits willy-nilly[6]. As people get on with the job of relating to each other within communities, so speech habits emerge which distinguish one from another. It is hardly surprising that a major cause of social division is manifesting itself as increasingly differentiated linguistic behaviour. Such developments are completely in line with historical anglophonic trends of *laissez faire* and *comme il faut*. But these natural developments, over which no conscious control has been exerted, appear to have gone unheeded in political discussions but may yet prove to have the most lasting consequences. That is why we all need to work hard now at ensuring that the measures for equality and anti-discrimination will be robust and well equipped to deal with such diversity as it evolves in the future.

The Next Symposium: 24-26 August 2001

We are delighted to be able to announce that there is to be a series of further symposia on *Language and Politics* which are to be held at Queen's University Belfast during the next three years from 2001-2003, in the first instance. The symposia are forming one of the 14 constituent research projects within the *AHRB Research Centre for Irish and Scottish Studies*, which is based at the Research Institute for Irish and Scottish Studies at the University of Aberdeen, and in which Queen's University Belfast and Trinity College Dublin are minor partners. The symposia are being organised jointly between ourselves and the Aberdeen University members of the committee of the Universities' Forum for Research on the Languages of Scotland and Ulster on the Forum's behalf.[8]

The dates have been set for the last weekend in August. Each symposium is expected to last from the Friday until the Sunday. The Symposium from 24-26 August 2001 will include invited presentations on the linguistic situation including linguistic rights in Switzerland and in Norway. In view of the September 2001 deadline for the submission of responses to the consultation document, there will be a session on Language Rights in the Northern Ireland Bill of Rights. Anyone interested in participating is welcome to contact us at Queen's University Belfast: <j.m.kirk@qub.ac.uk>, <d.obaoill@qub.ac.uk>.

Concluding Remarks

The Symposium brought together linguists and political activists, community workers and a government minister, statutory civil servants and journalists, politicians and interested members of the public. It was an unprecedented occasion of 'town and gown'. It created a tremendously strong sense of community and support and unity, which included the participants at the conference from all over the world as well as our particular guests from Scotland and the Republic of Ireland. We share the great optimism around politics in Northern Ireland right now, the feeling that real politics for the better is, at last, achievable, and that we each can make our contribution. We salute the courage and vision of the politicians who have made this possible and extend our strongest support never to let it go. Of course linguists define things differently from politicians, and of course linguists and activists will disagree over categories and distinctions, and each group will shout for their particular invested interest, but there is no doubt about the commonality of purpose and goal: if we each contribute what we can, constructively and responsibly, then Northern Ireland will be a better and more humane society: a multi-cultural or pluralist society with difference but equality, where each of us has the obligation to recognise, respect, understand and tolerate our linguistic diversity. We find the challenges ahead daunting but

exciting. **Through the symposia which we are organising, and through volumes such as the present, we are rising to them in our determination to give them our best shot.**

Notes

1. David C. Laycock, 'The status of Pitcairn-Norfolk: Creole, dialect or cant?'. In Ulrich Ammon (ed.) *Status and Function of Languages and Language Varieties* (Berlin: de Gruyter, 1989) 608-629.

2. John M. Kirk 'Ulster Scots: Realities and Myths', In *Ulster Folklife*. 44. 1998: 69-93.

3. This section was quoted by Kathryn Torney in her article '"We must move to tackle language needs"', *Belfast Telegraph*, 12.8.00, and summarised under the title 'Call for legislation over sexist language' in the 'For The Record' section of *The Times Higher Education Supplement*, 18.8.00.

4. We are grateful to the Women's Coalition and to colleagues at Queen's for their efforts in trying to find us a suitable spokesperson.

5. We are grateful to a number of politically active lesbians and to members of the Committee on Sexual Orientation (CoSo) for their efforts in trying to find us a suitable spokesperson.

6. We are also indebted to Pól Ó Muirí, Irish-language Editor of *The Irish Times*, for his presentation at the Symposium.

7. We regret that no Ulster Scots activist was able to attend.

8. The main study is Kevin McCafferty, *Ethnicity and Language Change* (Amsterdam: John Benjamins, December 2000). Scholarly articles include: Kevin McCafferty, 'Shared accents, divided speech community? Changes in Northern Ireland English', in *Language Variation and Change*. 10. 1998: 97-121; Kevin McCafferty, 'Barriers to Change: Ethnic Division and Phonological Innovation in Northern Hiberno-English', in *English World-Wide*. 19. 1998: 7-32. Cf. also John M. Kirk, 'Ethnolinguistic Differences in Northern Ireland', in Alan R. Thomas (ed.) *Issues and Methods in Dialectology* (Department of Linguistics, University of North Wales, Bangor, 1997) 55-68.

9. We are grateful to Tom Devine, Director of the AHRB Research Centre, and to Edna Longley and Cathal Ó Háinle, Associate Directors, for their support, and to Derrick McClure, Forum Chair, for his willing co-operation.

Ulster Scots: A Language? [1]

Manfred Görlach

Summary

Recent decisions recorded in the European Charter for Regional and Minority Languages and the Good Friday Agreement have given language status to Ulster Scots. However, this fact does not resolve the linguistic question of how far the variety can be properly regarded as autonomous, nor has it sparked off adequate discussion of the language-planning problems that the decision brings with it. In this paper, I will look at the situation in Ulster and compare the status and potential developments of Ulster Scots with similar situations in Continental Europe considering, in particular, Low German (including Grunnegers, 'the Groningen dialect of old Saxon') and Lëtzebuergesch ('Luxembourgish'), Swiss German and Romaunsh, Croatian and Serbian, as well as the diglossia in Jamaica.

1. Introduction

Now that Ulster Scots has been accepted in the European Charter as "one of Europe's 40 traditional minority languages" rather than as a dialect[2] The Good

---

[1]   My paper has profited a great deal from comments from colleagues more intimately acquainted with the situation than I, a Continental outsider, can be. I would like to thank in particular Jeff Kallen, John Kirk, Caroline Macafee, Aodán Mac Póilin, Colin Milton and Michael Montgomery. Many discussions at the conference have also helped me to see the implications of my topic much more clearly than I did before coming to Belfast. In the following discussion, I will use the term "Ulster Scots" for the historical spoken variety, reserving "Ullans" for the emerging written standard.

[2]   The European Charter for Regional and Minority Languages of 5 November 1992 does not specify the individual varieties covered by the act, nor does it define what a 'language' is. The commentary to the German edition states that in order to qualify varieties must be conspicuously different from the official languages, and therefore cannot be classified as dialects. However, it is nowhere defined in the document *how* different the varieties must be, since (it is admitted in the commentary) such a categorization includes psychological, sociological and political phenomena. It is therefore left to the authorities of member states to define the linguistic or attitudinal distance establishing an independent language. Ulster Scots is apparently understood as a 'variant' of the Scots language. At any rate, the Northern Ireland government is now committed to:
• Take resolute action to promote the Ulster-Scots language
• Facilitate and/or encourage the use of Ulster-Scots, in speech and writing, in public and private life
• Make provision for appropriate forms and means for the teaching and study of Ulster-Scots at all appropriate stages
• Provide facilities to enable non-speakers to learn Ulster-Scots if they so desire
• Promote study and research on Ulster-Scots at universities or equivalent institutions.

Friday Agreement leaves the status of Ulster Scots open:[3] The best survey of the moves that led from the founding of the Ulster Language Society and its claim to language status has also found a place in the 1998 Good Friday Agreement, my raising the question of its linguistic independence and autonomous status afresh, and doing so as an outsider with minimal expertise in the culture of the region (language, religion, economy or whatsoever), may seem somewhat out of place, or at least belated. However, I see the problem as one embedded in a wider European framework as well as in the context of, forgive my classification, 'Englishes', and have therefore accepted the conference organizers' kind invitation to speak on the topic. Needless to say, I have had to rely heavily on material made available by local collectors, and I welcome advice on anything open to question, on any of my judgments which seem unfair or mistaken.[4] I will quote extensively from commentaries in recent newspapers kindly supplied by colleagues, and I hope I will be able to interpret with approximate correctness the underlying political and other motivations in a forbiddingly complex situation.[5]

2.   Criteria for languageness

'Language' is admittedly one of the most difficult terms in linguistics (*word* and *sentence* are others). If we wish to relate the concept of language to the level of systematic functions and distinctions, a great number of criteria are available for a definition and, in consequence, for an allocation of a specific variety (or utterance) to the class of an individual 'language' (as opposed to [regional] dialect). In doing so I have repeatedly used a grid of parameters ultimately based

---

[3]   It states in paragraph 3:
> All participants recognise the importance of respect, understanding and tolerance in relation to linguistic diversity, including in Northern Ireland, the Irish language, Ulster Scots and the languages of the various ethnic communities, all of which are part of the cultural wealth of the island of Ireland.

The best survey of the moves that led from the founding of the Ulster Language Society in 1992 to the recognition of Ulster Scots as a minority language by the government of the U.K. in June 1999 is found in Montgomery (1999). A copy of this still unpublished essay was kindly supplied by the author after my first draft was complete in June 2000. Unsurprisingly, Montgomery's very balanced exposition exhibits some overlap with my paper.

[4]   I have to admit I was not fully aware of the virulence of the Ullans problem; that is why I failed to discuss the matter pro or con in my paper explicitly devoted to the correlation of language and nationhood (Görlach 1997). The German version is published in a collection of papers devoted to language and nation in a European context (Gardt 2000).

[5]   Montgomery perceptively points out the dangers of using such material in which language is sometimes employed as a loaded weapon when he says:
> Public discourse on the subject has sometimes been animated and acrimonious, often predictable and repetitious, but rarely has it been inquisitive, as views on Ulster Scots, including those of journalists, tend to rely on personal experience, preconceptions and attitudes (1999).

on Kloss's (1968) sociolinguistic definition. According to my classification, which I will apply to the problem under consideration, languageness is a matter of degree, defined by the extent to which the variety fulfils language-diagnostic criteria regarding the four a's: *viz.*, *abstand*, a term coined by Kloss to designate the structural distance of a variety from the nearest language on all individual levels, that is, phonology/graphematics, morphology, syntax and lexis; *ausbau*, functional range and degree of standardization; *attitude*, the self-perception of speakers and their willingness to be linguistically independent[6]; and *acquisition*, whether the variety was learnt as a mother tongue and has remained dominant for its speakers or not.

Further criteria have been offered which can be seen as complementary to these. Disregarding silly witticisms such as a "language is a dialect with an army and a navy", and not much more illuminating statements like "a language is a dialect with a dictionary, a grammar and a New Testament",[7] we may wish to add to the four a's Stewart's (1968) typology for successful language planning which is based on "standardisation, autonomy, historicity and vitality".

Stewart's paper was written with reference to "the new and developing nations", and if we accept for the moment that this qualification applies to Northern Ireland, we can see that his *standardization*, "the codification and acceptance of a formal set of norms defining 'correct usage', largely agrees with Kloss's *ausbau*. *Autonomy*, the function of the linguistic system as a unique and independent one" is less close, but close enough, to *abstand*. However, *historicity*, the fact that "the linguistic system is known or believed to be the result of normal development over time" is difficult to apply to our case; we might wish to say that it was the *borrowed* historicity of mainland literary Scots that kept Ulster Scots alive as a positively charged norm - in whatever restricted understanding. (On another level, trade, visits to relatives in Scotland, and frequent traffic across the water certainly helped to stabilize the use of everyday spoken Scots in Ulster). Finally, *vitality*, the use of the linguistic system by a non-isolated community of native speakers is always impossible to measure objectively in the case of coexisting related languages in which the minority form is drifting towards the structures of the higher, more prestigious variety. As a consequence, neither many utterances nor many texts can be unambiguously attributed to the one language system or the other, nor can the number of speakers of the minority language/dialect be counted. Frequently for the native speakers

---

[6] Attitudes are often expressed on matters which have little language in them, but are otherwise conspicuous. The provision of bilingual town- and street-name signs has been hotly debated in many multilingual communities. Press coverage on Ullans alternatives to traditional English streetnames in Co. Down has been extensive, and it was reported that in October 1999 in the East Belfast district of Castlereagh, a unionist stronghold, the plate with *Heichbrae Eirt* (translating *Tullyard Way*) was ripped down by loyalists (and therefore expected supporters of the move) who thought the words were Irish (*Irish News* 18/10/99).

[7] The claim has now been fulfilled, some might argue, with the publication of Fenton's dictionary (1995) and Robinson's grammar (1997), though for the New Testament Ullans readers will still have to make do with a few provisional passages in Robinson's *Grammar* (1997) and in *Ullans*, or go straight to Lorimer's Scots version (1983).

the distinction between the two becomes blurred or gets entirely lost. Stewart's grid (1968: 537) offers seven types of varieties based on his parameters (*viz.* 'standard', 'classical', 'artificial', 'vernacular', 'dialect', 'creole' and 'pidgin') but none of these provides a perfect match for Ulster Scots, so Ullans might come out as a type by itself.

Is there any point in considering the relative weight of the factors mentioned which might help bring us closer to an answer to the question in my title? Considered in detail and at close range we will soon discover that all arguments are relative, obviously depending on the individual sociolinguistic set-up. Thus:

1) *Abstand*[8] is neglected where members of a speech community decide that substantially divergent varieties (which may well not be intercomprehensible) should be considered one language; this can be for (possibly alleged) reasons of political, religious or otherwise cultural unity. Chinese is a much-quoted case - communication was (and largely still is) possible for many Chinese only in written form, because of the *abstand* between spoken varieties of, say, Shanghai and Canton, and the same holds, to a certain extent, also for Arabic. On the other hand, small differences between mutually intelligible varieties can be blown up in order to justify their classification as independent languages, again if there are political or religious reasons for such a decision. Serbian/Croat - and even Bosnian - are cases in question, and so are Macedonian/Bulgarian, Moldovan/Romanian and the Turkic languages of the former Soviet Union which were, for obvious political reasons, not regarded as dialects of Turkish. The title of Mencken's book *The American Language* of 1919 was meant as a provocation, and so was certainly Baker's title imitation *The Australian Language* of 1945, but it has to be admitted that in Noah Webster's times only a little effort in successful language planning would have been necessary for American English to constitute a new language - and thus implement Mencken's claim of 130 years later.

2) *Ausbau* may be a very European concept when used as a criterion for determining languageness - after all, most languages in the world do not seem to qualify because they have no writing systems, normative grammars or dictionaries, or their range of functions may well be restricted to informal spoken uses and employed for a limited number of topics □ and yet they count as languages by way of *abstand*. However, standardization and currency in 'respectable' written registers (possibly supported by historicity, that is, a written tradition, sometimes of a nostalgically upgraded past) certainly helps - and where it is lacking, it is comparatively easy to introduce norms by considered language planning, where the majority of the population still uses a non-standard variety - so to speak waiting for the linguist to make it regular and respectable, as in the case of Luxembourgish, which is natively spoken by some 95% of the country's

---

[8]   Kirk (p.c.) does not think that the equation of *abstand* = autonomy; *ausbau* = standardization works, at least not in the case of Ulster Scots.

population. However, we may wish to contrast the Jamaican decision *not* to expand the uses of Creole to formal written registers, although the native-speaker rate is alleged to be the same as in Luxembourg.

3)　*Attitude* is clearly the most important element in the set of factors mentioned; often emotional support by the speakers can override the fact that the distance to the nearest standard variety is minimal, and *ausbau* may be largely lacking. Even moribund and dead languages have occasionally been revived (admittedly, Ivrit is the only compelling example) and differences have intentionally been increased, as is happening in present-day Croatia, if there is enough support for such measures. The problem with utilizing supportive attitudes in the speech community, or even creating them, is clearly a political one. Do we want to fan existing nationalism by giving speakers an additional field for identification, and increasing the distance from neighbours, or worse, increasing internal division (see below)?

4)　*Acquisition* clearly comes into play where varieties are not learnt natively, or at least where the full range is not acquired as a native dialect in the home (perhaps not even from grandparents who, in some societies, can be used in revivalist programmes). The amount of second-dialect learning involved, and the language planning necessary in order to achieve the desired *ausbau*, result in various degrees of artificiality in language use. Such a situation may even create a parasitic variety which relies on the primary acquisition of the dominant language which is then relexified for identificational purposes as has happened in Anglo-Romani (and as in the efforts to extend the forms and functions of Scots currently) - a point which deserves special consideration and will be discussed later on.

3.　Are the contrasts of Scots and Low German and Scots and Jamaican useful parallels?

In two papers, I have drawn attention to the lessons that might be learnt about the status of Scots and consequent language planning by comparing the two bilingual or bidialectal speech communities that offer the most convincing similarities with mainland Scots. A detailed analysis of the social history of Low German (Görlach 1985) in the past five hundred years provides the most striking parallels to the situation of Scots.[9] The development for both minority languages is one of continuous erosion evident in:

---

[9]　I have here excluded cases in which the parallels are less striking, especially where the results diverge, such as in Swiss German (whose status as a dialect of German has never been seriously questioned) and Letzebuergesch (which did split off to form a fully codified standard language some twenty years ago; cf. the successfully preserved independence of Catalan).

1)   the loss of status and, finally, obsolescence as a written language (which in the case of Low German formerly even had limited currency as an international lingua franca);

2)   the loss of official domains (administration, schools and churches) and drastic reduction of the range of text types (for Scots cf. Görlach 1998);

3)   a restricted revival in selected literary genres from the 18th/19th centuries onwards - creating texts many of which even native speakers can now read only with the help of glossaries;

4)   the fossilization of linguistic structures and lexis on the basis of a pre-industrial period; a general failure to expand into new media (in written form, in newspapers, but also restricted uses of spoken forms in radio and TV);

5)   massive losses of dialect vocabulary and increasing formation of sociolinguistic continua replacing former diglossia, thus making modern Low German a stylistic option rather than a matter of codeswitching (that is, dialectalization); uncertainty among speakers about which code is being used (that is, mixture);

6)   20th-century efforts at revitalization of Low German in formal registers including written forms, and uses in the church and on radio and TV and (largely ineffectual) measures intended to create standard norms; the establishment of university departments and teaching in schools.

Although there is a great deal of linguistic awareness, and some institutional support, in Northern Germany, the decline of Low German has not been reversed; recent moves (such as the European Charter, and several MPs discussing the matter in Low German in the German parliament) have not stopped the erosion, or, to put it in a neutral way, the convergence, of the two related languages.

That this linguistic levelling is not restricted to Europe is clearly demonstrated by Jamaica.[10] Although the historical sources of the diglossia are quite different from the case of Low German, modern developments are not: there was never an early written tradition that declined over the centuries (as is the case in Scots) and a nostalgic looking back to a glorious past is not possible (since the focus would be on periods of slavery and social discrimination). However, the loss of distinctiveness (and thereby of diglossia) is the same as in Scots (a process which we may wish to call the dialectalization of a formerly independent language) as is the consequent lack of success in making Jamaican a standardized written language including formal registers.

What all these cases have in common is that most native speakers of minority languages are apparently convinced of the fact that competence in a language of wider communication and high prestige (German, English) is a valuable asset, and that the costs of successful language planning and subsequent

---

[10]   That the linguistic independence of creole languages is a possibility is demonstrated by, for instance, Krio (Sierra Leone) or Tok Pisin (Papua New Guinea); however, it is too early to say whether the development of a continuum is a possibility which would then be likely to be the precondition of a dialectalization of the creoles.

learning of a minority language is not justified if it has little more to offer than indicating national, regional or ethnic identity.

Looking back on the history of Scots over the past five hundred years, it is quite obvious that, with a few supporters of a standardized Scots language excepted, the pragmatic decision of its speakers was against such a codification. This applies most notably to the 18th century, when the language shift secured the Scottish Enlightenment a European audience as only Standard English could do (Latin being no longer available as a lingua franca for academic exchange). Such tendencies have of course gained in speed and thoroughness in a globalized world - whatever language enthusiasts think about the issue.

4.   The revival and revitalization of minority languages

As remarked above, the standardization of a vital minority language such as Luxembourgish is not a technical problem, although successful implementation of the new norm in official functions may well be. Revival and revitalization are, however, quite a different matter, and any such attempt is likely to profit from the study of earlier case histories. As far as Britain is concerned we may therefore wish to look at neo-Cornish (or neo-Manx) on the one hand, and at Irish on the other.

Since Cornish died a quiet death, as an impoverished rural language, more than two hundred years ago, its pronunciation must be reconstructed, and its lexis, if it is to be adequate for modern requirements, has to be complemented by thousands of new words, either borrowed from English or coined from native bases. The artificiality of the process is all too apparent, even if we were to accept - and few people would - that the revival makes sociolinguistic sense. The revitalization of Irish appeared to be much more promising, since there were probably fewer than 10 percent of native speakers left in the country when Irish was made official in 1922, and the language issue was strongly supported by a feeling of national identity after independence, and seen as contributing to national unity (rather than internal division). However, it would be far too optimistic to describe the Irish language planning of the past eighty years as a success story. Not only is the range and frequency of uses of the language still very limited, and the number of native speakers down to 10,000 and still declining, but the grammatical structure of Irish is increasingly influenced by the dominant English. Critical observers see many modern Irish utterances as relexified English, speakers neglecting the unique syntactical structures of authentic Irish.[11] It has been repeatedly pointed out that Irish had all the institutional and financial assistance that its supporters could have wished. Looking further afield, we find that the story of the Romaunsh languages

---

[11]   Drastic changes in present-day Irish are admitted by all observers, although the role English has had in the process is still being debated. Some think that most grammatical changes have come from an internal process of simplification (Mac Póilin, p.c.) - a traditional dilemma in contact linguistics.

(dialects?) in Switzerland is quite similar. Although the Swiss government has given Romaunsh full recognition and a great deal of financial assistance, it appears that the language shift to the bigger language, German, cannot be stopped. The situation of such minority varieties may ironically become worse once a written standard is introduced. This is normally intended to stabilize the language by giving it a wider range of functions and raise its prestige - but is then often not accepted as a norm by 'their' native speakers (who of course speak a local dialect rather than the newly created standard form).

The dangers involved in revitalizing minority languages genetically related to the dominant standard language are even more conspicuous. These have often become dialectalized in a stylistic continuum, having come to occupy the informal end of the sociolinguistic cline. Decisions aiming at re-constituting their historical linguistic independence must necessarily concentrate on increasing *abstand*. In the case of Low German, Scots or 19th-century Yiddish this has normally meant avoiding lexical items shared with the major language and preferring a distinctively regional alternative - whether still in (limited) use, or revived from older sources such as classical authors, or coined by translation (in the case of Scots either by translating the English/neo-Latin item, or copying a solution offered by another Germanic language such as Norwegian or German). The problem here is that there is no surviving speech community with unalloyed stylistic competence (or *sprachgefühl*) capable of judging the adequacy of the linguistic experiments offered by the author in his language-planning efforts.

5.   The demographic and sociohistorical position of Ullans

The debate about Ulster Scots (conveniently named by the newly coined term Ullans to give it more weight) in the 1990s came as a surprise to the linguistic world. Introduced by Scottish settlers of the late 16th/early 17th-century plantations, Ulster Scots came under the influence of English varieties from the beginning (cf. Montgomery 1991) or, to put it another way, it started merging with them. As happened to dialects in other parts of Europe, the variety was somewhat protected by rural isolation in pre-industrial societies, and even had an attitudinal and partly literary revival in the 19th century. However, not supported by institutional backing and social prestige, it seemed to be dying a quiet death, retreating even more quickly than its mother-tongue Scots in mainland Scotland. This at least is how I interpret the results of Gregg's investigations of the 1960s and subsequent reports. At best, it was a tongue in hiding - O'Toole (1996) refers to the fact-finding commission[12] which failed to find native speakers, so that "the world was not made aware of its existence until the Ulster Scots Society was formed in 1992". Such judgments, it is important to restate, do not depend on whether there are still 100,000 or 150,000 speakers of it, but rather relate to the

---

[12]   O'Toole's reference to a "fact-finding commission" is inaccurate; each member of the group compiled an individual report, and the standing of the group and the findings were somewhat misrepresented in some accounts in the nationalist media (Mac Póilin, p.c.).

quality of their Scots. Has it not gone the way of more or less most half-languages and dialects in modern Europe, becoming impoverished lexically[13] and being ultimately reduced to accent features? How distinctive is the speech of its speakers? How many people are unmistakably Scots by way of pronunciation (like Ian Paisley or David Trimble) but probably incapable of keeping up a conversation in Ulster Scots? Is the situation really different in rural Ards or, separated by a political border and therefore even more protected by relative isolation, in the Donegal Scots communities? To an external and possibly underinformed (but well-wishing) observer, the reports of a study visit looking for native speakers of Ulster Scots, but unable to produce them (however partisan the 'findings' sound), have a certain familiarity - since they have parallels in other parts of Europe. (I grew up in a part of Germany classified as Low-German speaking, but do not remember hearing a single word of it back in the 1950s).

What we appear to need urgently is a large-scale sociolinguistic investigation of the Ulster Scots speech community, if there is such an entity, replicating the painstaking research of Gregg for the modern age. Details that must be established are:[14]

1)   What degree of broadness, especially in lexis and grammar, is still left among Ulster Scots speakers, and how consistently is the vernacular used in informal situations?

2)   How acceptable among its speakers are functional extensions into more formal registers (such as administration, education, and the church), or even the codification of written norms? Do speakers really want to have their informal variety standardized □ and are others willing to learn it, and for what reasons?

3)   What chance is there of implementing such decisions if they are supported by a substantial portion of the population?

6.   The codification and elaboration of Ullans

A half-language, according to Kloss (1968), is characterized by linguistic impoverishment and reduced functions (which normally go together with reduced prestige). However, it would be a grievous mistake to think that to supply a reduced variety with written genres such as expository prose, and enrich its

---

[13] It is important to point out that collections of the hamely tongue, which comprise a majority of words only remembered by old people and many relating to industries and farming procedures long obsolete cannot be adduced in a discussion about languageness (cf. Malcolm, *News Letter*, 9/4/1999).

[14] Compare the list of desiderata drawn up by Montgomery (1999) who names seven topics for empirical research (core territory and diagnostic features; variation; sociolinguistic profile of the speech community; attitudes; relationship with English as a continuum or diglossia; history; obsolescence). Such data would help us to make more reliable statements on the present status of Ulster Scots than are possible today.

lexicon, would automatically raise its status to that of a full language. I admit to have made such an error of judgment when I saw a parallel between the status of 16th-century English and modern Scots - and asked J.K. Annand to translate Mulcaster's programmatic "Why not all in English?" (1584) into "The state of Scots" (in McClure, ed. 1981:6). The mistake is, of course, that the 'Luxembourgish' situation of Early Modern English, when the non-standard form was still spoken by all, cannot be equated with a state in which only a certain proportion of speakers are left[15], that is, the position of Scots in Scotland and of Ullans in Ulster.

However, if the *ausbau* of Ullans is envisaged (and some activists would say, there is now no choice), the technical procedure is not controversial. Language planners, in theory, will be able to describe the necessary steps in agreement with well-established principles:

1)   Code selection will have to define what kind of Scots is to be the norm variety. The basis of this is likely to be a 'pure' variety as traditionally preferred by dialectologists who believed in the unadulterated speech of the non-mobile older rural males, the proverbial NORMs; this will possibly be complemented by prescriptive ideas derived from the historical Scots language - that of Scotland. Whatever the choice, this would effectually make the new standard a language without native speakers - even before the next steps were taken.

2)   In order to equip Ullans for modern functions, elaboration has to take place especially in the lexicon - and there are in fact conspicuous developments in that direction in modern written Ullans, even though these are clearly still experimental.

3)   Implementation, supporters of the cause might wish to claim, is now safeguarded by the European Charter, and guaranteed in tandem with moves to expand the uses of Irish in Northern Ireland. However, it is difficult to believe that, whatever the degree of enthusiasm and official support (if it ever came to be), Ullans could be re-established in the community as a fully fledged language in all registers.

Features of neo-Scots can be determined from the experimental uses of the 1990s. The artificiality the newly created written standard is evident from the few Ullans texts that have been produced □ texts that are almost totally unknown outside Northern Ireland.[16] The character of the lexicon, the most conspicuous element, has been convincingly analysed by Kirk (see this volume). I agree with him in the dangers of the enterprise. Lexical elaboration means that words are either revived from older Scottish texts and, more often than not, given new meanings for modern contexts, or are coined from properly Scots elements. The result is clearly

---

[15]   As a consequence, we decided to leave out the portion when the collection of statements was reprinted in *Focus on: Scotland* (Görlach 1985:181-202).

[16]   Compare Montgomery's warning: "Efforts at writing by enthusiasts will no doubt have limitations and excesses, and it is unfortunate that some of these are taken as THE language" (1999).

similar to what drew Jonson's criticism on Spenser's diction, when he stated "Spenser, in affecting the ancients, writ no language." The difference is, of course, that Spenser was creating a poetic style appropriate for the literary genre of pastoral poetry, and thus intentionally distanced his style from other forms of contemporary English. But such an aim cannot be the intention of the Ullanists.

The elaboration of the lexicon can, then, proceed on at least five levels:

1)   dialect terms can be adopted for standard purposes, especially those that have parallels in English, Irish and possibly mainland Scots;

2)   archaic diction can be revived or (what comes to the same effect) words can be taken from the literary tradition and re-employed in 'secularized' functions.

These two solutions, for all the disconcerting changes in stylistic labels, would at least not be too obviously 'concocted', a danger which is, by contrast, obvious for:

3)   new derivations and compounds made from native Scots elements, often as loan translations from neo-Latin/Greek (such as *langbletherer* from *telephone*) or German (such as *stoursucker* from *Staubsauger* 'vacuum cleaner'). The entertainment value of such formations is high, and sometimes there is even a suspicion that such proposals are slyly made by opponents of the cause in order to damage it[17];

4)   new loanwords, including Latin and French, not shared by English, thus continuing a tradition dating back to at least the period of the Auld Alliance. There is less chance, or danger, of independent borrowing from Irish to enrich the Ullans vocabulary (excepting the considerable number of Gaelic words already contained in Ullans dialects);

5)   new meanings, especially with old and respectable Scots words to make them serve to designate modern objects and ideas - possibly the least offensive way of lexical expansion.

Distancing Ullans from English brings with it dangers replicating earlier attempts aimed at similar objectives. More than 200 years ago, Geddes warned with regard to the Scottish poetry of his times:

> Thus, to write Scottish poetry ... nothing more was deemed necessary than to interlard the composition with a number of words and trite provincial phrases, in common use among the illiterate; and the more anonymous and farther removed from the polite usage those words and phrases were, so much the more apposite and eligible they were

---

[17]   The point is excellently brought out in a letter to the editor in the *Irish Times* of 1/3/99, where John Arden takes offense at the translation of *director* as *heich heid yin*: "What on earth is the matter with *director* as a legitimate Ulster-Scots word?" After all, Lyndsay called his work *Ane Satyre of the Three Estaits, in commendation of vertew and vituperation of vyce,* "commendation, not *gude speich frae a lustie mou*, and vituperation, not *ill speich frae a sair wame*, or any other such kailyard clatter."

accounted. It was enough that they were not found in an English lexicon to give them a preference in the Scottish lexicon. (1782:403, quoted from Jones 1995:17-8)

Such problems have increased in modern times rather than become less relevant. McClure rightly points to the restricted acceptability of puristic coinages:

> One of the reasons for the limited degree of acceptance won by the new Norwegian language is that an unrealistic attempt was made to purge it of foreign borrowings - including the internationally-used words from modern technology that are found in nearly all contemporary European languages. Of course Scots writers should be perfectly at liberty to invent new forms if they wish to do so: as Douglas Young, for example, concocted *light-bumbazit* for *dazzled*, *keethanlie* for *apparently*, *ice-flume* for *glacier*, *flownrie* for *fragile*, *owreset* for *translate*, and *thraipfu* for *famous*: but far from being necessary it would probably be extremely harmful to carry this principle to any length as a matter of official policy. (1980:28)

A related problem has to do with the de-intellectualization of neo-Ullans. Since the variety more or less stopped expanding in the 18th century (as other European non-standard forms did), a translator into Ullans can either produce a naive-sounding paraphrase or stay very close to English. The down-to-earth directness of dialect speech was playfully brought out by Barnes (1886) in his translation into the Southwestern dialect of the queen's speech. If such de-intellectualized language is promoted to be a standard, it invites sneers; if by contrast it is raised to the abstraction of full modern languages, it loses the connection with the native speakers (who, being bidialectal, have always used St E for formal purposes).

If we wish to summarize language planning results so far, Ullans is linguistically to be categorized as what Laycock (1989) has called a 'cant', that is, a second dialect relearnt to stress ethnicity and largely parasitical since competence in it largely depends on the prior acquisition of another language of wider communication, English. Discussing the language situation on Norfolk Island, he found that the Pitcairn descendants cultivated their linguistic identity by implanting into the dominant Australian English of the majority of Norfolk residents a few hundred lexical items of their ancestral speech. The dividing line between such enriched varieties and proper secret languages such as Anglo-Romani is narrow. Here again, we have a parasitic language depending on the primary acquisition of English into which, at teenage, Romani items are implanted - with pronunciation, morphology and syntax remaining totally English.

In all these cases ethnic or group identity is highlighted by linguistic distance, and it seems that this clearly is also the motivation behind the efforts towards an Ullans Movement - at least among its activists.

7.   The political implications

William Branford, in his preface to his *Dictionary of South African English* (Branford 1987) explained why he wisely refrained from providing ethnic labels in his entries. He argued that categories like Black English (apart from the uncertainty of such ascriptions in individual cases) might be in the way of a future South African society, whose chance lay, and still lies, in unity and compromise rather than in the internal divisions so long cultivated by apartheid governments.[18] There is, I think, a lesson here for Ulster. The historical orientation of many, though certainly not all, people in Northern Ireland, in relating present-day conditions to a pre-plantation Celtic country or the Scottish settlement of the early 17th century and the Battle of the Boyne respectively, is difficult for foreigners to appreciate. The argument that Ulster Scots is older than insular Celtic which goes under the concept of *Cru(i)thin* (cf. Adamson 1974 and 1998) and, independently, *the tribe of Dan* (cf. Robinson 1998), is even more difficult to understand.[19] Accordingly, the re-introduction of Irish - a language that has not had any native speakers in the region for at least one generation - and the Unionists' response in form of the promotion of Ullans are strangely different from what is happening in most other parts of Europe. It is remarkable that the question of mainland Scots as indicated above has (until very recently) never played a part in the political programme of the Scottish National Party (although we might argue there is a much stronger justification for such a demand), and that political division has raised the question of Ullans being accepted as a language - as a variety shared with Scotland, where its status is less vociferously stressed?

The question, then, remains whether Ullans is seen as a dialect of a greater Scots language (thus the European Charter) or whether it should be considered entirely independent. The latter claim is not as absurd as it sounds at first hearing. Politically, it might be more acceptable than forming part of a greater Scots speech community, which would stress the links with Great Britain. There is some speculation that the German dialects in Alsace and Lorraine would have fared better if a Luxembourgish solution had been found for them - that is, a status in between French and German.[20] Independent Ullans, however tenuous its

---

[18] "There is no systematic labelling for 'Black', 'Afrikaans', 'Coloured' or 'Indian' provenance. In the first place these varieties flow into one another ... Furthermore, labelling of this kind is likely to be counter-productive if any kind of 'General South African English' is ever to come into being." (1987:xiii-xiv)

[19] As Montgomery (1999) rightly cautions, Ian Adamson's and Philip Robinson's works should of course be read the way the authors intended. I am here concerned with the dangers of their texts becoming misused as parts of political manifestos. For instance, during summer 2000, there appeared in Protestant East Belfast a wall mural claiming self-confidently that Ullans is 4000 years old.

[20] The closest possible parallel to Ullans in a European context is the Low Saxon of the province of Groningen, known as Grunnegers, being most closely related to (a dialect of?) the Low German of North Germany, which itself has an endangered language status, to say the least, as against Standard High German. However, Grunnegers, despite some literary use including various translations, has apparently not seen any national(istic) revival and therefore fails to provide a proper parallel to Ullans.

acceptability, might also at least be easier for language planners to construct since they would probably have to deal with a more homogeneous entity than a pan-Scots (including everything from Shetland to the borders).[21] Moreover, their decisions at codification (especially in spelling and lexis) would not have to be agreed upon with Scottish authorities - who have been trying to find a solution for standard spelling for generations. Proceeding rapidly with the functional expansion and standardization of Ullans could even have an impact on decision-making in Scotland - one way or another. It is likely that sober Scotsmen might for instance learn from the reactions produced by the advertisement for an Equal Opportunities Manager in four languages, a term which in Ullans came out as an *Eeksie-Peeksie Skame Heid-Yin* and was widely discussed, or rather ridiculed, in newspapers in late 1999.

As I have tried to show in detail in (1997), linguistic nationalism has never played an important role for varieties of English, when it came to active language planning to establish *ausbau* and increase *abstand* from St E in order to use the newly standardized form as a badge of national or ethnic identity. For all the support it had from a large section of its speakers and at least tolerance by the majority, American Black English (Ebonic, Black English Vernacular, Afro- or African American English) was never standardized and actively promoted as is proposed for Ullans. On a national level, Canada, Australia and New Zealand are well-defined speech communities, with clear identities, with no need to stress the linguistic distance from British English, or international English. This illustrates the fact that there are many possibilities of documenting your difference without using conspicuously divergent languages and that, if your identity is to be expressed linguistically, accent features like Canadian Raising, quasi-Cockney in Australia or, for that matter, centralization of diphthongs on Martha's Vineyard, will serve the purpose.

---

[21] Again, for varieties of mainland Scots, written conventions have more or less been accepted for Shetland, Northeastern and Glaswegian urban dialects; deciding on an acceptable spelling and vocabulary was of course much easier for these individual dialects than for a standard comprising all the regional forms of Scots. It is needless to add that this gives local writing much more authenticity (and, thereby, acceptability) than an anaemic standard that is nobody•s native tongue. Compare, in this context, Trudgill's statement on literacy in Scots:

> We can also hope and work for a future where Scottish children will be able to write their native dialects in all situations. This is not a plea, incidentally, for the use of Lallans. (For many Scottish children this would be just as much an alien standard that they would have to learn anew as standard English). (quoted by Low in McClure *et al.* 1980:84)

Note that written Grunnegers is conspicuously different from other forms of Low German by employing spelling conventions derived from Dutch rather than German.

8.   The present discussion in Northern Ireland (1996-2000)

How do an outsider's reflections relate to the present discussion in Northern Ireland? Given the importance of speakers' attitudes in deciding which variety is a language, and which is a dialect, a linguist, basing his judgment on objective criteria such as *abstand* and *ausbau*, cannot tell members of a speech community that they have, possibly, taken an unconvincing decision. The speakers of Ulster Scots have to decide on the matter, and I cannot pontificate and tell them they are wrong.[22] However, it would be good to have it made clear that arguments pro and con are either based on alleged historical facts (in which case, many of those quoted are wrong or at least misleading) or on attitudes, and therefore politically motivated. If political considerations form the basis of the decision, then the fact should be openly admitted. The impression an outsider gets is one of a highly politicized discussion which, being waged by people often insufficiently aware of historiolinguistic and sociolinguistic facts and methods, seems to have created more heat than light.

For speakers who love their dialect and want to hand it on to the next generation(s), the question of dialect vs. language does not arise. And in fact, regional, national or ethnic identity can lead to a reversal of the tendency of dialect erosion, as the example of German-speaking Switzerland in the 20th century beautifully illustrates - and this development is happening under our eyes - without Swiss speakers claiming they speak Switzerlandish rather than German. It is typical that arguments for the preservation of Ulster Scots such as those listed by one observer do not relate to the question of languageness; all are at least as applicable to dialect conservation (about which there is no controversy): Ulster Scots, it is said,

> does express and articulate a rural community cohesion and has a role
> to play in opposing the decimation of rural communities. It is used by
> at least one very good amateur drama group. It enshrines the radical
> political thinking of James Orr and his contemporaries of 1798 and as
> such it is a historical and education resource. It is a rich repository of
> Gaelic words which it has observed ... It is the natural medium of
> some beautiful songs. It is necessary for the understanding of many
> placenames. It is a cross-community dialect and not the property of
> any one faction. (*Irish News*, 28/9/96)

But for Northern Ireland it is apparently too late for such reflexions being useful. The legal consequences of a decision which gives language status to Ullans and parity of esteem with Irish have created a situation in which people who still insist on raising the question of languageness can be compared, as another commentator polemically did, to "the linguistic equivalent of the Flat Earth

---

[22]   If the majority of speakers consider their speech a dialect of English, the Scots element in it making up the distinctive element that serves for regional identity, then this linguistic basis seems to be fully sufficient for the purpose.

Society" (*Belfast Telegraph*, 4/12/98). As many language planners have found, all will now depend on successful implementation. How is language planning going to succeed if, as the journalist Lara Bradley stated, "Despite a tiresome trawl through the civil service, not a single fluent Ulster-Scots speaker could be found to take up a £19,000 post translating Assembly proceedings into Ulster Scots" (quoted in *News Letter*, 6/4/1999)? How successful will be the attempts to convince non-Ullans speakers that their speech is more than just a "DIY language for Orangemen"? How will the, say, 100,000 speakers claimed for Ulster Scots react to its being standardized and taught in the schools? Will any speakers outside the speech community decide to learn Ullans, and for what purpose? Will the community be satisfied with the present status which, according to the European Charter, does not give Ullans quite the same status as Irish □ but which now channels more money into the preservation and modernization of Ullans than the language societies for mainland Scots can dream of? Is the Ulster Scots situation really "Past tense, but future perfect" as the journalist Ian Malcolm stated using a nice linguistic joke in April 1999 (*News Letter*, 7/4/1999)? The problem is ironically that it has happened so quickly and with less effort than is commonly connected with getting language rights for a community. Political developments have created a slot that now needs to be filled overnight. There has not even been the time for extensive studies of the Ulster Scots speech community to investigate their linguistic self-perceptions and attitudes towards a coming standard language. The necessary steps will need to be taken with great caution. All steps undertaken towards an *ausbau* of Ulster Scots should be carefully discussed with representatives of the dialect community (such as teachers, parsons, folk singers and other linguistically competent people) to find out whether proposed solutions will be accepted by the native speakers. 'Solutions' that by-pass them (which would result in their not recognizing Ullans as 'our' language) are the worst possible — and other cases show that such developments are a real danger. Even modern Ullans writing, experimental as it still is, is a serious warning: an artificial written form without speakers, which also leaves the intended speech community without a written norm related to their dialect. Human experience makes one doubt the likelihood of a successful revitalization, which would be in many respects, effectively a new creation of a variety which in principle deserves all our sympathy and support □ though possibly it should be protected against its all too ardent supporters. I could not do any better than to quote Mac Póilin's well-balanced statement (made of course before the legalization of language status for Ullans):

> The fact that Ulster Scots does not have the same kind of secure linguistic status as Irish does not diminish its value one whit. Ulster Scots needs support, as does every effective measure to restore dignity and confidence to the communities that still speak it. (*Belfast Telegraph*, 2/12/1998)

In sum, the situation presents itself as a vicious circle: if potential motivation is the decisive factor for a success of the standardization of Ulster Scots, then we cannot really want it to succeed because the move is divisive; if, on the other hand, Ullans is hoped to be accepted by all members of the community, then it loses the political push and is in consequence likely to disappear quite soon again as a written language.

References

Adamson, Ian. 1974. *The Cruthin*. Bangor: Pretani Press.

Adamson, Ian. 1998. Dalaradia: *Kingdom of the Cruthin*. Bangor: Pretani Press.

Barnes, William. 1886. *A Glossary of the Dorset Dialect with a Grammar*. Dorchester: Case; the queen's speech is reproduced in Görlach (1999:212).

Branford, William. 1987. *The South African Pocket Oxford Dictionary*. Cape Town: Oxford University Press.

Fenton, James. 1995. *The Hamely Tongue: A Personal Record of Ulster Scots*. Newtownards: Ulster Scots Academic Press.

Gardt, Andreas, ed. 2000. *Nation und Sprache*. Berlin: de Gruyter.

Geddes, A. 1792. "Three Scottish poems, with a previous dissertation on the Scoto-Saxon dialect." *Transactions of the Society of Antiquaries of Scotland*. Edinburgh 1:402-68.

Görlach, Manfred. 1985. "Scots and Low German: the social history of two minority languages". In Manfred Görlach. ed. *Focus on: Scotland*. Amsterdam: Benjamins, 19-36.

Görlach, Manfred. 1991. "Scotland and Jamaica - bidialectal or bilingual?" In Manfred Görlach. *Englishes: Studies in Varieties* of English 1984-1988. Amsterdam: Benjamins. 69-89.

Görlach, Manfred. 1997. "Language and nation: the concept of linguistic identity in the history of English." *English World-Wide* 18:1-34.

Görlach, Manfred. 1998. "Text types and the history of Scots." In Manfred Görlach *Even More Englishes. Studies 1996-1997*. Amsterdam: Benjamins, 55-77.

Görlach, Manfred. 1999. *English in 19th-Century England*. Cambridge: University Press.

Görlach, Manfred. 2000. "*Nation* und *Sprache*: das Englische." In Gardt, 613-41.

Jones, Charles. 1995. *A Language Suppressed. The Pronunciation of the Scots Language in the 18th Century*. Edinburgh: John Donald.

Jones, Charles. ed. 1997. *The Edinburgh History of the Scots Language*. Edinburgh: University Press.

Jones, Charles. 1999. "Nationality and standardization: the English language in Scotland in the age of improvement." *Sociolinguistica* 13:112-28.

Kirk, John M. 1998 [appeared 2000]. "Ulster Scots: realities and myths." *Ulster Folklife*, 44:69-93.

Kirk, John M. 2000. "Two Ullans Texts" (this volume)

Kloss, Heinz. 1968. *Die Entwicklung neuer germanischer Kultursprachen seit 1800*. Düsseldorf: Bagel. Second Edition.

Laycock, Donald C. 1989. "The status of Pitcairn-Norfolk: Creole, dialect or cant?" In Ulrich Ammon, ed., *Status and Function of Languages and Language Varieties*. Berlin: de Gruyter, 608-29.

Lorimer, W.L. 1983. *The New Testament in Scots*. Edinburgh: Southside.

Macafee, Caroline. 1981. "Nationalism and the Scots Renaissance now." *English World-Wide* 2:29-38.

Macafee, Caroline. ed. 1996. *Concise Ulster Dictionary*. Oxford: University Press.

McClure, J. Derrick. ed. 1981. "*Our ain leid*? The predicament of a Scots writer." *English World-Wide* 2:1-18, abbrev. reprint in Görlach 1985.

McClure, J. Derrick. 1988/1997. *Why Scots Matters*. Edinburgh: Saltire Society.

McClure, J. Derrick, *et al*. 1980. *The Scots Language. Planning for Modern Usage*. Edinburgh: Ramsay Head.

Montgomery, Michael B. 1991. "The anglicization of Scots in 17th-century Ulster." *Studies in Scottish Literature* 26:50-64.

Montgomery, Michael B. 1999. "The position of Ulster Scots." *Ulster Folklife*, 45: 86-107.

Montgomery, Michael B and R.J. Gregg. 1997. "The Scots language in Ulster." In Jones, 569-622.

Robinson, Philip. 1989. "The Scots language in 17th-century Ulster." *Ulster Folklife*: 35-86-99.

Robinson, Philip. 1997. *Ulster-Scots: A Grammar of the Written and Spoken Language*. Belfast: Ullans Press.

Robinson, Philip. 1998. *Wake the Tribe o' Dan*. Belfast: Ullans Press.

Stewart, William. 1968. "A sociolinguistic typology for describing national multilingualism." In Joshua A. Fishman, ed. *Readings in the Sociology of Language*. The Hague: Mouton, 531-45.

Recent newspaper articles and similar sources

Arden, John. 1999. "Language or dialect?" *Irish Times* 1/3/99.

Bradley, Lara. 1999. "*Mind your language*: Ulster-Scots movement 'scunnered'" *News Letter* 5/3/99:17.

Kennedy, Billy. 1999. "Celebrating a 'language' that simply doesn't exist."

Kilroy, Ian. 1999. "Blether and Babel." *Sunday Tribune* 27/8/99.

McCausland, Nelson. 1998. "Living tongue must be shown respect", *Belfast Telegraph* 4/12/98.

MacLochlainn, Brian. 1996. "The guid guide to finding that elusive 'Ulster Scots'", *Irish News* 28/9/96.

Mac Póilin, Aodán. 1998. "Words apart." *Belfast Telegraph* 2/12/98.

Malcolm, Ian. 1999   (a) "A case of irritable vowel syndrome",
                      (b) "Past tense: but future perfect",
                      (c) "It's a *tongue* - so stick it out." *News Letter*, 6-9/4/99.

McKeen, Bab. 2000. "Aye til tha Ulster-Scotch leid."

Myers, Kevin. 1999. "An Irishman's diary." *Irish Times* 12/2/99:15.

O'Toole, Michael. 1996. "Ulster Scots 'language' rubbished." *Irish News*, 11/9/96.

Ryder, Chris. 1999. "Ulster-Scots will trip off tongue soon as minority language." *Irish Times* 13/5/1999.

Sharrock, David. 1996. "'DIY language' fails to impress." *Guardian*, 12/9/96.

Two Ullans Texts

John M. Kirk[1]

1. Introduction

'Ullans' can be thought of as revivalist attempts to expand traditional dialect with neologisms and other innovations, to extend the dialect to new registers, and to perceive the new dialect in the new registers as a new written 'language' in its own right: 'Ullans', which is not English. Let us investigate.

2. Two Texts

The two texts chosen for analysis are translations of texts originally in English and which were simultaneously published: (a) an information leaflet on employment by Belfast City Council, and (b) a job advert issued by the Northern Ireland Office. Leaflets and job adverts traditionally belong to the standard dialect. These are reproduced in a specially edited parallel-text version in which the sentences are numbered; **the Ullans versions are in bold;** *the English versions are in italics.*

Text 1

Bilfawst Citie Cooncil ... inlats fur ilkaboadie
Belfast City Council ... Opportunities for Everyone
<1> **Cud ye compluther we iz - yer ain sel?**
Does your face fit?
<2> **Gin ye'r taakin o inlats fur darg wi Bilfawst Citie Cooncil, tha repone wud be 'ay'.**
When it comes to employment opportunities with Belfast City Council, the answer is 'yes'.
<3> **Bilfawst Citie Cooncil - aareddie wi mair warkers nor near onie ither boadie in tha citie - is ettled fur tae hae its inlats o darg apen til aaboadie.**
Belfast City Council - already one of the city's biggest employers - is committed to making sure that its employment opportunities are open to everyone.
<4> **Nae metter quhar ye'r frae, an quhitiver fawks ye caa yer ain, sae lang as yer the tap boadie fur tha jab, ye wud compluther wi iz richtlie!**
Whatever your background, whatever community you come from, if you are the best person for the job, your face fits!

<5> **We tak fowks on fur bein tha maist fit fur tha darg, an haein tha richt exams an siclike, sae gif ye houl ye'r on fur yin yae jab, we wud be blythe fur ye tae pit in fur it.**

We recruit on the basis of ability, qualifications and aptitude for work so if you think you could handle a particular post we would welcome your application.

<6> **Tha Rax til Resydenters Ettlin wuz drew up fur tae skail thon thocht til aa oor resydenters sae as tha maist feck o aa soarts o fowk wull pit tharsels forrit fur jabs wi Bilfawst Citie Cooncil**

The Community Outreach Programme has been designed to take that message to all our communities so that jobs within Belfast City Council will attract applications from the broadest possible base ...

<7> **... quhilk airtins shud gie a heeze til tha Citie Cooncil's ettlin on preein the tap boadies fur tha richt jabs.**

... which will help the City council to find the best people for the best jobs.

<8> **Gin ye jalooze yer ain resydenter yins cud get tha guid o preein mair anent jab inlats wi Bilfawst Citie Cooncil gie tha Rax til Resydenters Kemper a blaa on Bilfawst (01232) 270404 or a faix on Bilfawst (01232) 239988.**

If you feel your community could benefit from finding out more about employment opportunities with Belfast City Council then contact The Community Outreach Officer by telephone on Belfast (01232) 270404 or fax us on Belfast 239988.

<9> **We cu gie oot wittins scrievins, set oot wittins boords or set up a wee taak.**

We can supply information packs, an information display or arrange a talk.

<10> **Gin ye cud dae wi a haun wi owresettin or hae a need o by-ordinar wittens, we wud be blythe tae gie a heeze.**

If you need help with translation or require specialist information we will be happy to help.

<11> **Jist spier.**

Just ask.

<12> **Syne, we hae gien a throu-gaun til a wheen o tha spierins maist aften pit anent warkin fur Bilfawst Citie Cooncil ...**

In the meantime, we have looked at some of the most frequently asked questions about working for Belfast City Council ...

<13> **aiblins ye hae tuk tent o thir daeins yersel ...**

perhaps you have wondered about the same issues ...

<14> **A dinnae taak Inglis guid. A jalooze frae that I wudnae hae muckle chaunce o a jab?**

I don't have good English. I suppose that means there is no real chance of a job for me?

<13> **Aiblins no.**

Not necessarily.

<14> **Fur some jabs, richt eneuch, ye maun hae guid Inglis fur taakin and scrievin no thaim aa bot.**

Some jobs do of course require fluency in both spoken and written English, but not all.

<15> Gin ye binnae fit tae fill in tha jab inlat paiper, we wud be blythe tae ettle on giein ye a haun oorsels, or pittin ye on tae someboadie at can.

If you have difficulty in completing an application form we will be happy to try to assist you or to put you in touch with someone who can.

<16> Wud tha Citie Cooncil be 'guid bosses'?

Is the City Council a 'good employer'?

<17> Ay, sae we maintain richt eneuch.

Yes, we certainly think so.

<18> Bilfawst Citie Cooncil bis a bien spat tae dae yer darg wi strand an feckfu ettlins anent wark in guid staunin wi tha Dargers Claucht.

Belfast City Council has good working conditions and strong and effective employment policies agreed with the Trades Unions.

<19> Tha Citie Cooncil gart fur tae wark wi 'maist guid airtins' in ilka pairt o employmenn.

The City Council is committed to working to 'best practice' in every area of employment.

<20> Luk at tha guid ettlins we hae agin deavin ither wi dirtie or pairtie taak, an we hae ettle on giein tha ae inlat o chaunce fur ilkaboadie nae metter o quhit sex ye ir, quhit kirk or pairtie ye houl wi, yer leid, gin ye be cripplelt, or hae ocht ither wrang wi ye, or onie ither sic daeins.

This means, for example, that we have firm policies against sexual and sectarian harassment and we actively work towards providing equal opportunities for everyone irrespective of gender, religion, marital status, political opinion, race, disability or any other such matter.

<21> Gin Bilfawst Citie Cooncil bis sic a guid boss quhit wud it hae pit oot tha Rax til Resydenters Ettlin fur?

If Belfast City Council is such a good employer why has it launched The Community Outreach Programme?

<22> We houl it wudnae be eneuch jist tae be apen til aa wi oor jab foarms; we maun skail thon wittens oot til aa fowks an kittle aaboadie tae tak up tha inlats gien.

We feel it isn't enough simply to be open to applications from all communities; we have to take that message out to people and actively encourage everyone to take advantage of the opportunities offered.

<23> Soons guid, saw quhit wye wud A get a jab?

Sounds great, so how do I get a job?

<24> Jabs wi Bilfawst Citie Cooncil is pit oot in tha *Belfast Telegraph, Newsletter* an *Irish News* an wi tha Training and Employment Agency.

Jobs in Belfast City Council are advertised in the Belfast Telegraph, News Letter *and* Irish News *and or through the Training and Employment Agency.*

<25> Ye wull be gart fill oot a jab inlat foarm, an, gin ye hae tha richt needs o tha jab ye will be shoart-listit an gien an invite fur tae cum alang tae a spierin panel o thie fowk ats haein perfait trainin fur takin tha pick.

You will be asked to complete a standard application form and, assuming you meet the relevant criteria for the job, you will be short-listed and invited to come along for interview by a panel of three people who are fully trained in recruitment and selection.

<26> **Gin ye'r no tuk up at tha furst, dinnae let that pit ye aff frae haein anither go.**

If you aren't successful the first time, don't let that stop you from trying again.

<27> **Cud A pit in fur ocht ava wi a C.V. jist?**

Can I apply 'on spec'; by sending in a cv?

<28> **Naa, feard no.**

Unforunately, no

<29> **Sae as we aye be perfait fair an hannle aa foarms tha yin wye, ilka boadie maun pit in fur jabs tha yin road.**

In order to be completely fair and to process all applications systematically we require each applicant to apply by completing a standard application form.

<30> **Wud thar be monie jabs gaun wi Bilfawst Citie Cooncil?**

Are there many jobs on offer in Belfast City Council?

<31> **Ay, tha Cooncil bin yin o tha Citie's maist muckle employers wi mair nor 2,300 fu dargers.**

Yes, the Council is one of the city's biggest employers with more than 2,300 permanent employees.

<32> **Hooaniver, thar wudnae be monie fowks leein iz - aiblins sein as we'r sic guid bosses - an thar wudnae be monie jabs gaun neist yeirs, bot ilka yin o thae maun be an inlat fur someboadie.**

However, there isn't a high turnover of staff - we like to think that's because it's a good organisation to work with - but there are many vacancies during the course of an average year and every one of those vacancies represents an opportunity for someone.

<33> **Wud that be aa soarts o jabs?**

Is there a big range of jobs?

<32> **Ay. We hae hunners o dargers at aa pairts o tha citie frae heich heid yins til keepers at tha azoo, quhilk gies guid licht o aa tha Cooncil maun dae.**

Yes. we have literally hundreds of posts at locations throughout the city, from administrators to zoo-keepers, reflecting the Council's responsibilities.

<33> **A jalooze ye maun hae a degree tae git a stairt?**

I suppose you need a degree to get a foot in the door?

<34> **Fur maist jabs, naa. Fur quarthie poasts ye maun hae college exams an ither jab airts.**

For most jobs, no. Some posts do require academic qualifications, specialist vocational skills or aptitudes.

<35> **A hae a hame tae luik efter: quhit wye cud A dae that an dae a jab wi tha Cooncil at tha yin time?**

I have family commitments; how could I combine those with a job with Belfast City Council?

<36> **Bilfawst haes a hale wheen o 'hameart heezin' ettlins.**

Belfast City Council has a range of 'family friendly' policies.

<37> **Wi monie a tha jabs ye can pick tha hoors tae suit. We hae mittherin heeze holidays, plons fur twa sharin tha yin jab, an career breaks.**

In many posts there are flexible working hours. We have maternity support leave, job sharing schemes and career breaks.

<38> **A hae a disabilitie: Wud that rule me oot?**

I have a disability; will that disqualify me?

<39> **Fur certes naa. We wud gie a fair faa til yer jab inlat foarms an ye'll pree at, wi that Citie Cooncil, we aareddie hae wrocht wi a guid ettlin wi disabilitie, oor 10 point plan Plon Fur Guid Ettlin.**

Absolutely not. We will welcome your application and you will find that, within the City Council, we already have in operation a strategy on disability, our 10 point Agenda For Positive Action.

Text 2

The New Northern Ireland Assembly
Office of the Official Report (Hansard)
<1> **Unner-Editor (Inglis an Ulster-Scotch) fur tha Chaummer o tha Scrievit Account (Hansard)**
Sub-Editor (English and Ulster-Scots) in the Office of the Official Report (Hansard)
<2> **6-month leemited-tairm contraick, Sellerie: £13,737 tae £19,215**
6-month fixed-term contract, Salary £13,737 to £19,215
<3> **It's noo apen fur tae pit in jab foarms fur tha ontak i Unner-Editor (Inglis an Ulster-Scotch) wi tha Chaummer o tha Scrievit Accoont (Hansard) o tha New Ulster Semmlie sittin at tha Tolsel Biggins, Stormont, Bilfawst.**
Applications are invited for the post of Sub-Editor (English and Ulster Scots) in the Office of the Official report (Hansard) of the New Northern Ireland Assembly, which is located at Parliament Buildings, Stormont, Belfast.
<4> **A start wull be gien fur sax month, wi anither contraick aiblins forbye.**
The appointment will be for six months, with the possibility of renewal of contract.
<5> **Yin ats pit in fur it maun hae GCSE/GCE 'O' level Grade A or B fur Inglis Leid, or less a like exam taen an hauden tae bear the same gree or abain. Aa thir maun be wi iz afore tha hinmaist day an hoor gien.**
Applicants must possess GCSE/GCE 'O' Level Grade A or B in English Language, which must be obtained by the closing date for applications, or relevant formal qualifications considered to be of an equivalent or higher standard.
<6> **Ilka yin on tha leet wull be gart sit a sey piece fur tae kythe: a perfit guid hannlin o tha Inglis, takin in gin yer fit or no fur tae owreset the wurds spake intil aisy read scrievin, houlin tha much ye can o tha taakeris ain wyes an gates; a guid braid kennin; an a unnerstaunin o daeins anent parliament an pairty ettlins, maist o aa adae wi Norlin Airlann; an a guid hannlin o tha Ulster-Scotch leid.**
Candidates will also be required to demonstrate, by way of an aptitude test: a thorough command of English, including the ability to turn the spoken word into

easily readable narrative, retaining as much as possible of the speaker's style and idiom; a wide general knowledge; and an understanding of parliamentary and political affairs, with particular reference to Northern Ireland; and proficiency in Ulster-Scots.

<7> **Yae jab form a mair wittins, like tha jabs ontaks forbye tha ither things ye maun hae afore getting waled, cannae be gat wiioot scrievin (giein jab nummer PB 3/99) til Recruitment Service, Orchard House, 40 Foyle Street, Londonderry, BT68 6DJ.**

An application form and more detailed information, including the duties and responsibilities of the post as well as the further criteria to be used in the selection process, may be obtained only by writing (quoting job reference number PB 3/99) to Recruitment Service, Orchard House, 40 Foyle Street, Londonderry, BT48 6AT.

<8> **Filled in jab foarms maun be wi iz afore 26th February 1999.**

Completed application forms must be returned to arrive not later than 26th February 1999.

<9> **The Semmlie wull be gye blythe fur tae get jab foarms on tha leet pit in wi onie weel-fitted boadie nae matter thair kirk, sex, ills, race, quhit pairtie ye houl wi, aild, merriet or no, or sexual airt.**

The Assembly welcomes applications from all suitably qualified candidates irrespective of religion, gender, disability, race, political opinion, age, marital status or sexual orientation.

<10> **Ilka jab forms wull be preed anent abilitie an naethin else ava.**

All applications for employment are considered strictly on the basis of merit.

[from *Belfast Telegraph*, 9.2.99]

3. General Characteristics

An informational leaflet and a job advert are not only the registers for the new written dialect; others include scholarly articles on history and a newspaper article dealing with preventive medicine in the future. Most texts are translations, showing a dependency on an original text in English.

On the basis of these texts, general characteristics of the new written dialect are emerging: they show a revival of obsolete words, neologisms deploying Germanic patterns of word-formation, and lexical invention. At the same time, they show an avoidance of abstractions and of Latinate diction. Invention extends beyond the creation of new lexical items to include new senses and new semantic functions for existing items in English. The intention behind these neologising strategies is both to create an impression of familiar colloquiality, to make it sound like something that would actually be spoken, and, at the same time, somewhat contradictorily, to differentiate the dialect from written English. The net effect of an amalgam of traditional, surviving, revived, changed, and invented features, is artificial dialect. It is certainly not a written version of the vestigial spoken dialect of rural county Antrim, as its activists frequently urge, perpetrating the fallacy that it's *wor ain leid*. (Besides, the dialect revivalists claim *not* to be native speakers of the dialect themselves!). The colloquialness of this new written dialect is deceptive for it is neither spoken nor innate. Traditional dialect speakers find it counter-intuitive and false (although that may not be unrelated to the use of the dialect in new register situations). Letters to the *Belfast Telegraph* along these lines are expressing descriptively justifiable views. The ultimate intention behind these revivalist efforts is to show that the dialect is no dialect of English but a separate language in its own right: *Ulster-Scots* or *Ullans* (see Görlach in this volume). What those rural farmers and others who still speak the traditional dialect consider themselves to be speaking is, to them, 'English', a variety of 'the English language', neither a language that is separate, nor a language that is 'Scots'. Nobody speaks the language of the job advert or the council leaflet because many of the expressions have never existed in the traditional dialect to be spoken.

The new written dialect raises many issues. Traditional spoken dialects of Scots are essentially 'sociolects' and have been shown to express social, educational and economic characteristics of the speakers. Spoken varieties of Scots are sociolects as well as dialects in so far as their use is limited by social class or by social aspirations as well as by geographical space. In brief, present-day Scots dialects including that in Northern Ireland are varieties used by working class speakers, in the spoken mode, in informal situations within their own homes. Now here lies a potential conflict. In formal situations, the characteristics of the speaker tend to become foregrounded over those of the message, so that it is hard to avoid the interpretation that written dialect is working class speech written down. By comparison, written standard English comes across invariably as being socially neutral and, because of this, as being capable of all or any thought. In traditional dialect poetry, poetic rhetoric suppresses social class connotations, but innovative Scottish poets like Tom Leonard have exploited both rhetorical and orthographic conventions to show that the speaker is a working-class Glaswegian, *just wanna u scruff tokn*, thus showing unmistakably that message cannot be divorced from the messenger, or that the message is directly related to the messenger's cognitive and communicative abilities: *this is ma trooth*.

Nevertheless, the artificiality and counter-intuitiveness of this new written dialect go some way towards suppressing social identifications. It is doubtful whether readers of these texts associate the content with any social characteristics of a particular speaker. Rather, the combination of structural artificiality, on the one hand, and of subject matter, situation of use (register), and, following on from that, seriousness of purpose, and formality of tone, on the other, all seem to avoid social class identification and any concomitant stigmatisation. Artificiality and counter-intuitiveness militate against social association.

4. Structural Features

Let us now consider some specific features. In these two texts, there are many lexical words which are simply respelled to indicate local accent, e.g. in the nouns: *abilitie* ('ability'), *contraick* ('contract') *foarm* ('form'), *jab* ('job'), *pit* ('put'), *tairm* ('term'), *sellerie* ('salary'), *soart* ('sort'), *spat* ('spot'), *taaker* ('talker'), *unnerstaunin* ('understanding'); in the proper nouns: *Semmlie* ('Assembly'), *Bilfawst* ('Belfast'), *Norlin Airlann* ('Northern Ireland'); in the verb forms: *gien* ('given'), *hae/haein* ('have'/'having'), *pit* ('put'), *taen* ('taken') and *hauden* ('held'); in the adjective: *aisy* ('easy'); and in the adverb *aareddie* ('already'). All these English words are respelled within the conventions and habitual associations of the English spelling system so as to represent and be interpreted as indicative of certain pronunciations, presumed to be characteristic of a Scots accent.

For grammatical words, respellings have long existed, as in the prepositions: *fur* ('for'), *tae* ('to') *wi* ('with'); the number *sax* ('six'); the auxiliary verb *wull* ('will'), the article *tha* ('the'); the conjunction *an* ('and'); the pronouns *iz* ('us') and *naethin* ('nothing'); the determiners *ain* ('own'), *anither* ('another') and *maist* ('most'). These, too, are all English words which are respelled to indicate a phonic value and appropriate interpretation.

One bizarre feature of the dialect spelling is the obsolete <quh-> forms for the voiceless bilabial fricative as in English *wh-* forms and last used productively in the early seventeenth century; thus 'who' becomes rendered as *quho*, 'which' as *quich* or *quilk*. Although a salient marker of late medieval Scots, its borrowing into the present system has proved unpopular because its opaqueness denies it its intended functionality within the overall spelling system of English. Rather, its motivation has been symbolic: the indication of the archaic Scottishness of the dialect, as well as furthering the maximisation of difference from other forms of written English.

Traditional dialect vocabulary occurs in the nouns *airtins, darg, feck, leet* ('list'), *a sey piece* ('aptitude test'), *spierins* ('questions'); in the proper nouns *Chaummer* (cf *City Chambers* or 'Town Hall') and *Tolsel* ('Parliament'); in the verbs *jalooze* ('feel', 'suppose'), *kittle, kythe* ('demonstrate'), *pree, compluther, skail* ('take'), *spier* ('ask'); in the adjectives *bien* ('good'), *by-ordinar* ('specialist'), *feckfu* ('effective'), *quarthie* (form of *twarthie* from 'twa-three' meaning 'several'); in the adverbs *abain, afore, aiblins, ay, forbye, hinmaist*, and *less a like*; in the grammatical items: *maun, yin,* and in the expression *yin yae jab* ('a particular post'). These words range from being obsolete to ongoing use in current speech, although obsolete words remain in the passive vocabulary. The function of these words is to extend the referential range of English either by extending the range absolutely or by substituting equivalent expressions in English with an added sense of local cultural identity shared with Scotland generally and not peculiar to Northern Ireland.

Germanic patterns of word-formation can be seen in lexical choices such as *waled* (for 'selected') and in words involving a participle and verbal noun with a dynamic but general meaning can be seen in: *inlats* ('opportunities'), *ontak* ('post', also 'duties and responsibilities'), *owreset* ('turn' and also 'translate'), *takin in* ('including') *tak on* ('recruit'), *throu-gaun* (as in *gien a guid throu-gaun tae*) ('to look at'); also in the participle *unner-* in *unner-editor* for 'sub-editor'. This patterning of word formation in the standard dialect was interrupted by the intervention of Norman French, without which many more such Germanic patterns would have been at the centre of the standard vocabulary today. Avoidance of Romance and classical diction provides further help towards maximising difference from English.

Because so much of the new written dialect has to be invented, some words become semantically overworked: *airt* ('orientation'), the verb *ettle* as in *ettle on giein ye a haun oorsels ...*, *ettled* ('committed'), and the noun *ettlin* as in *ettlins* ('affairs', 'policies' and 'programme') as in *tha Citie Cooncil's ettlin*, the causative modal verb *gart* ('is committed to'), and the verbs *get* and *gie* with its various complements as in *get tha guid o preein tuk tent o ...* ('wondered'), *gie a heeze til ...* ('to help ...'), *gie x a blaa* ('to phone'), *gie oot* ('to supply'), *gie a throu-gaun til ...* , the verb *tak* ('to recruit'), and the nouns *wyes an gates* ('style and idiom').

In addition to vocabulary, these texts reveal some traditional dialect grammatical forms, as in the verb suffix *-it* (*scrievit*) (although the standard form is retained in 'filled in'); the absence of number marking with a temporal noun, as in *month* ('months'); the use of the *fur-tae* complementiser, as in *fur tae kythe* or *fur tae skail thon thocht ...* ('to take that message ...'); the modal behaviour of the causative verb *gar*, as in *gart sit*; the use of the prepositions *anent* and *til*; the use of *yae*; the *get* passive as in *getting waled*; the presence of *-in* verbal participle forms (except the instance *afore getting waled*); the indefinite pronoun *ilkaboadie* ('everyone'); the replacement of the present perfect with the simple past tense as in *wuz drew up in ...* ('has been designed ...'); the relative pronoun form *at*; the durative uses of finite *be* and its negated form *binnae*.

In terms of structural indices of orthographic, morphological and lexical forms, the individual features are all analysable either as realisations or exponents of structural and functional variants or as the variants themselves within the respective overall subsystems of English. Remove the 'funny' spelling intended to represent the local accent, and an English word appears. None of these forms, individually or collectively, amount to arguments about separate language status; rather, they are real or invented dialect variants within the overall English system, and depend on that system for their value and interpretation.

5. Stylistic Features

Some features of these texts are stylistic rather than structural. There are numerous instances of the avoidance of abstractions, with different solutions. Examples of direct word-for-word substitution include the following nouns: *maist guid airtins* ('best practice'), *jab airts* ('specialist vocational skills or aptitudes'), *exam* ('qualifications') (cf. *college exams* for 'academic qualifications'), *a hame tae luik efter* ('family commitments'), *inlat o chaunce* ('equal opportunities'), *inlats fur darg*, *inlats o darg* ('employment opportunities'), *jab foarms* ('applications'), *resydenters* (the 'community'), *a start* ('the appointment'), *sexual airt* ('sexual orientation'), and *thocht* ('message'); the following verbs: *hae* ('possess'), *hauden* ('considered'), *be gart* ('be required'), *houlin* ('retaining'), *gat* ('obtained'), *giein* ('quoting'), *fill in* ('complete'). Some two word verbs: *gie oot* ('supply'), *rule oot* ('disqualify'); the following phrases: *get tha gui o* .. ('benefit'), *hae a need o* ('require'), *maun hae guid Inglis* ('require fluency'), *dae at the yin time* ('combine'); the following adjectives: *fu* ('permanent'), *nae matter* ('irrespective'); the following adverbs: *the yin wye* ('systematically'); and the prepositional phrase *adae wi* ('with reference to').

Some abstract nouns are replaced with dynamic verbal nouns: *daeins* ('issues' and also 'affairs'), *hannlin* ('command' and also 'proficiency'), *kennin* ('knowledge), *aisy read scrievin* ('easily readable narrative'), and *wittins* ('information').

Replacement of words with a general noun or pronoun and a defining relative clause include: *yin ats pit in fur it* ('applicants'), *ilka yin on the leet* ('candidates'), *tha much ye can* ('as much as possible'), *forbye tha ither things ye maun hae* 'the further criteria') *quhit kirk ... ye houl wi* ('religion'), *quhat pairtie ye houl wi* ('political opinion'), and *quhar ye'r frae* ('background').

Some postmodifers are reduced finite clauses, as in: *hinmaist day an hoor gien*, ('closing date') and *the words spake* ('the spoken word').

Other clausal substitutions include: *gin yer fit or no* ('the ability'), *gin ye be cripplelt* ('disability'), *merriet or no* ('marital status'), *bein tha maist fit fur tha darg* 'ability'), *haein tha richt exams an siclike* ('qualifications and aptitude for work'), *and we wud be blythe fur ye tae pit in fur it* ('we would welcome your application'). In one clause, both the grammar and the polarity are reworked: *binnae fit tae ...* ('have difficulty in ...').

These stylistic features are not relevant for an adjudication of the new written dialect as a language separate from English, as revivalists urge, or, as shown here, as yet another dialect of English. Rather, they serve to reinforce the colloquiality and informality of each text, giving the impression that the the text is a written version of something originally spoken. They are markers of spontaneous, informal, unplanned thought, not markers of carefully prepared and revised, edited, depersonalised formal writing.

6.   Translation Features

Some features of these texts arise from their status and quality as a translation. Translations are about referential equivalence, but certain translations raise doubts: English 'sex' is translated as *gender* in the dialect, but are they referentially equivalent? Or English 'religion' with dialect *kirk* (in Scots, traditionally, the *Kirk* is the Protestant and specifically Presbyterian Church.); 'community' with *fawks* (cf. *quhitiver fawks ye caa yer ain* with 'whatever community you come from'); 'the best person' with *the tap boadie*; and 'a good employer' with *guid bosses*? The English conjunction 'if' is sometimes rendered as *if*, but it is also rendered as *gif*, *gin*, *when*, and *sae lang as*, not all of which express conditionality. To 'take advantage of something' is not the same as *to take up something*, and *something tuk up* need not be 'something successful'. The translation of certain technical terms does not suggest equivalents: are *tha hoors tae suit* the same as 'flexible working hours'? 'Leave' is not 'holiday', so is 'maternity support leave' identical with *mittherin heeze holidays*? And if 'schemes' are not 'plans', are 'job sharing schemes' *plons fur twa sharin tha yin jab*? 'Good working conditions' are not implied by *a bien spat tae dae yer darg*. There is no notion of 'pack' when 'information packs' is rendered as *wittins scrievins*. Other terms have been invented: *Inglis Leid* for 'English Language' as school subject, *Dargers Claucht* for 'Trades Unions', although it suggests a collective, whereas 'Trades Unions' is plural. The formal neutrality of 'sexual or sectarian harassment' is not rendered by the derogatory informality *deavin ither wi dirtie or pairtie taak*, nor that of 'an interview panel' with *a spierin panel*.

The authenticity of the translation may be challenged on other grounds. English grammar disallows the construction *it's open to put in applications* on the grounds that the subject of the embedded clause cannot be inferred from the main (or control) clause. In the dialect sentence *It's noo apen fur tae pit in jab foarms* ... it is just as impossible to infer the identity of that subject.

In the expression *yin ats pit in fur it*, I read *ats* as a reduced form of *has* contracted to a reduced form of *that*, although the expression may have been intended as *yin at pits in fur it*, whereby the *-s* is a third person inflection.

Further challenges come from the modality system. Throughout all dialects of English, the assertion of a case is surely invariable. Yet the present tense is translated by the epistemic modal *would* as in ... *tha repone wud be 'ay'* ... the answer is 'yes'; ... *ye wud compluther wi iz richtlie!* '...your face fits!' *Wud tha Citie Cooncil be 'guid bosses'*? 'Is the City Council a "good employer"'? And the distribution of modal adverbs also raises the question of epistemic equivalence, as with *aiblins no* as a translation of 'not necessarily', *richt eneuch* for 'certainly', and *fur certes naa* for 'absolutely not'. These translations raise further difficulties with referential equivalence. The phrase 'with the possibility of renewal of contract' implies that the contract may be renewed, whereas the dialect rendering *wi anither contraick aiblins forbye* refers to a new contract. In the English version, the O-level qualifications must be obtained by the closing date for applications, whereas in the dialect version, by the closing date for applications, it is the application giving details of the O-level qualifications which *maun be wi iz*.

Separate points are made about Belfast City Council between 'already one of the city's biggest employers' and *aareddie wi mair warkers nor near onie ither boadie in tha citie*. To 'agree with someone' is not the same as *to be in guid staunin wi someone*.

The four items 'marital status, political opinion, race, disability' are not adequately translated by *gin ye be cripplelt or hae ocht ither wrang wi ye*, nor are these and other examples politically correct, with implicit discrimination and intolerance.

Some words are translated by English synonyms rendered with dialect spelling, as in: *account* ('report'), *leemited* ('fixed'), *sittin* ('located'), and *taaker* ('speaker') no doubt in furtherance of the strategy to maximise difference. There are dialect replacements for other English words: *repone* (for 'answer'), *houl* (for 'think'), *to be on fur* (for 'to handle'), *a wheen o* (for 'some'), *muckle* (for 'large') and *maist muckle* (for 'biggest').

7.   Conclusion

Although the words of these translations are intended to represent Ullans as a language system separate from English, a close analysis of these texts in terms of their various structural and stylistic features and of their translation quality shows that Ullans is nothing other than a set of departures from the overall linguistic system of English, with variable quality and success. The features are variants of English features, or realisations or exponents or these variants. There are no major differences of system or structure. Traditional features co-occur with innovations and creations. Both co-occur in turn with common words which have undergone semantic or functional change and consequent re-interpretation. Synonymic variants co-exist with English variants in the same synonymic sets. The achievement of these texts is a new *destandardised* or *non-standardised* dialect of English, which is being used, in these texts, to communicate information in a formal written register. It is therefore hardly surprising that it should follow that two varieties of the same overall language system are unable to say 'the same thing'. Within the same system, two expressions of 'the same thing' will inevitably contrast referentially, or stylistically, or in the value of their social interpretation. Far from these texts representing the traditional Co. Antrim spoken dialect written down, or a new standardised dialect of Scots, these experiments in Ullans are shown to be composed of lexical features, whether revived or invented, which are extensions or, departures from, the overall system of English. In short, Ullans is an artificial amalgam, which is ultimately *English* all the same. *A tongue nae man ne'er spak.*

.

Note

1   I am grateful to Magnus Ljung for allowing me to pre-publish a revised version of this paper originally intended to appear as 'The New Written Scots Dialect in Present-day Northern Ireland', in M. Ljung (ed.) *Linguistic Variation and Change: A Festschrift for Gunnel Melchers* [Almqvist and Wiksell, Stockholm] Stockholm Studies in English

Northern Nationalists and the Politics of the Irish Language: The Historical Background

Liam S Andrews

The Anglicisation of Ireland and Depoliticisation of Irish

During the 16th and 17th centuries, the experience of oppression and dispossession shared by the Catholic native Irish and the Catholic Old English brought both parties together. The focus for this development was the Catholic seminaries of Europe where the elites of both communities were educated (Cunningham 1986: 166; Ó Buachalla 1993: 15). This began a process of identity shift amongst the native Irish which aligned them with the Counter-Reformation whose main priority in the Three Kingdoms was to combat English-speaking Protestantism. As Clarke (1978: 68-70) has pointed out, the most natural leaders of this project in Ireland were the Old English, whose standard of civility was closest to the European norm. Whole-hearted native Irish commitment to the same project made the acceleration of anglicisation unavoidable.

Under the influence of the Counter-Reformation, native Irish scholars at home and abroad reinterpreted Irish history to make Catholicism the focus of a new national identity (Cunningham 1989: 29-30; Ó Buachalla 1993: 14-23). This brought the native Irish and Old English together in the service of Rome. According to Ó Buachalla (1983: 106), this newly-created Irish Catholic identity was incompatible with the native Irish way of life, and consequently the latter was marginalised before the end of the century. Literacy (primarily in English) soon became an important indicator of civility uniting Protestants and anglicised Irish Catholics in a common culture and leading the latter to despise the illiterate Irish-speaking population (Barnard 1993: 271).

According to Walsh, writing in 1713, English was now the most common and prevailing language (of the literate); the study and use of Irish had been laid aside or discouraged since the introduction of printing, and parents preferred to have their children educated in English rather than Irish (Harrison 1988: 33-34). Irish had become the insignificant vernacular of the lower orders (Williams 1986: 129).

Its insignificance helped to depoliticise the language. Earlier it had been associated with native subversion and savagery but proselytism, contacts with native scholars, and academic interest in England and beyond had kindled an Ascendancy interest in the language and Irish antiquity (Barnard 1993: 270; Leerssen 1986: 321-331).

During the 17th and 18th centuries, literary and scholarly output continued within the Irish-speaking population. However, although literature in Irish flourished during this time, it did not keep pace with the changes in society and ultimately withered in the early 1800s. What continued was largely an oral tradition (Ó Háinle 1994: 749). Continuity in the scholarly tradition of Irish-speaking society could be found in the scribal activity that flourished during the

18th and 19th centuries (Harrison 1988: 24; Ó Conchúir 1982: 224-27). From 1750 onwards, the amount of English in MSS increased and, towards the end of the century, phonetic spelling became more common, suggesting a reading knowledge based on English (Cullen 1990: 21-22, 32). By the 1830s, there were few good scribes left (Ó Conchúir 1982; 229).

The Catholic church leadership and most of its clergy were recruited from English-speaking communities (Ó Ciosáin 1997: 119, Ó Buachalla 1983: 96). Official church documents in Irish were few and little was done to publish the many devotional works that existed in MSS form at the time (Ó Cuív 1986, 380). As the new Tridentine model of the church began to take shape from the mid-18th century onwards, English was the language of its developing structures and devotional practices. That included the Catholic school system, which grew after 1782 (Ó Ciosáin 1997: 119, 167; Ó Tuathaigh 1986: 122).

By the end of the century, middle class Catholic families had turned to English and used Irish to communicate with the rural peasantry. All those who were educated, or knew the value of education, identified Irish with poverty, backwardness and lack of opportunity. English was identified with progress. Irish was seen as a dying language soon to be replaced by English (Ó Tuathaigh 1995: 13-14).

Negative attitudes towards the language intensified in the decades after the 1798 Rebellion, when Protestant evangelicals began to use it extensively in a renewed effort to convert the Catholic population (Durkacz 1983: 118-122). Apart from preaching, the Protestant evangelical crusade included an organised attempt to make Irish speakers literate in their own language so that they could read the bible (De Brún 1982-83: 281-282).

Early Stages in the Politicisation of Irish

In the sectarian atmosphere engendered by the struggle for emancipation and the evangelical onslaught on Catholicism, the Irish language was politicised. Catholics saw literacy in Irish as a potential threat to their religion and sense of community (De Brún 1982-83: 285). Controversies provoked by the efforts of evangelical organisations to teach literacy in Irish encouraged the abandonment of literary activity in Irish and the rejection of the language itself.

During this period there was an important shift in Catholic thinking. Implacable anti-Catholic prejudice had made conciliatory arguments seem pointless and humiliating. Confrontation became more attractive. The majority spurned the notion that the government should be given influence in the affairs of their Church in return for Catholic relief (Bartlett 1992: 293-295; Connolly 1989a: 44). They had developed a shared consciousness which attached particular importance to the Church as a national institution and were affronted that it should be contaminated by anti-Catholic British influence. This reaction, according to Bartlett (1992: 294), was the first major expression of Irish Catholic nationalism in the 19th century.

Catholic militancy was further enhanced by the religious controversy associated with the Protestant evangelical crusade. The Catholic clergy joined the fray, and soon there was great hostility and community tension as these battles moved into the political arena. By this stage, the Catholic peasantry had become intensely politicised, sectarianised and conscious of its strength (Bartlett 1992: 311; Connolly 1989b: 74-79). They enlisted in their thousands in the Catholic Association in 1824 under the leadership of Daniel O'Connell. Organised by local clergy, they helped create such a powerful pressure group and political machine that the government was forced to grant Catholics emancipation in 1829 or face the danger of rebellion or civil war.

The Catholic clergy had played a key role in events. As spiritual and community leaders faced with the threat of militant Protestantism in both the spiritual and secular worlds, they had become political leaders. Catholics were now a united powerful political force capable of undermining Protestant hegemony in Ireland. Irish history had reached a turning point. A Catholic nation had emerged whose identity had been formed by opposition to, and hostility from, Protestants (Bartlett 1992: 337-442; Connolly 1989b: 84-88, 102-106).

Emancipation followed as the British sacrificed ideology to pragmatism and a fundamental change in the British constitution resulted. Simultaneously the Catholic Church began to develop as a major power bloc in Ireland. This development, according to Inglis, was facilitated by English politicians who realised that it alone was capable of bringing British norms of civility to a potentially rebellious Irish population (Inglis 1987: 120-121; Inglis 1991: 58).

Wright (1996: 49-50) also observes that the shared trauma of those with a Catholic identity in Ireland made the despised religion rather than the despised language (as was the case in other European countries) the focus of a new nationalist ideology and ethnic consciousness. For Irish Catholics, theological rather than linguistic boundaries became ethnic boundaries. From their perspective, to be Catholic was to be Irish, and to be Protestant was to be alien.

Irish Language and Catholic Identity in the mid-19th Century

Changes in social attitudes put Irish in a negative light. As Victorian norms of middle class respectability and civilised behaviour developed during the 19th century, supported by increased religious conservatism amongst Irish Catholics, the Irish language tended to be identified with the moral laxity and the unacceptable social customs of a past age which should be discouraged (Ó Tuathaigh 1986: 130-135; Connolly 1982: 191-3).

The massive expansion of Catholic church infrastructure that occurred after emancipation to cater for the educational, health and social needs of the Catholic community achieved three things: (1) it revolutionised the nature of Catholicism in Ireland; (2) it offered Catholics 'native' norms, models and routes to civility in opposition to those provided by the alien Protestant British state; and (3) it created its own network of institutions rivalling those of the state (Inglis 1987: 120-125, 203-204). In fact, as long as the ethos of the British state remained Protestant, the Catholic church functioned virtually as a state within a state, protecting its own. However, both shared the same anglicising dynamic.

Locally, the Catholic chapel became the focus of religious practice, and church discipline dominated Catholic community life. At the centre was the priest, who represented and led his community, and who reached an unrivalled position of power (at least in rural areas) from the late 19th century onwards. These Catholic clergy, who came mostly from rural backgrounds, promoted unquestioning obedience to Church teaching and a protective communalism that supported familial and social conformity (MacMahon 1981: 279). This protective Catholic communalism was reinforced by Protestant hostility.

Since emancipation the majority of Protestants, motivated by fear, had done what they could to oppose the advance of Catholic power.   As democratisation spread under central government and older colonial control structures decayed Protestants (especially in Ulster) found themselves sharing territory with increasingly assertive self-organised Catholics.

Conservative Protestants felt threatened in two ways: by Catholic religious self-organisation, and by Catholic political self-organisation.   The first, they believed, subverted the Protestant nature of the British state, and the second threatened their very lives.   Their solution was to challenge both on every occasion and thus make their paranoia a reality (Wright 1996: 18-20, 48, 52, 56, 97, 151, 155, 274, 339-340).

In support of their actions, they gradually transformed Protestant theological ideas into a settler ideology which focused on the inherent inferiority and unsavable nature of the native Catholic population; their unmitigated enmity towards Protestants and Protestantism; the relationship of every self-organised Catholic action to the one master-conspiracy – the destruction of both Protestantism and Protestants; the absolute justification of continued Protestant supremacy in Ireland to maintain civilisation; and the need for pan-Protestant vigilance and solidarity to counter Catholic self-organisation (Wright 1996: 20, 69, 280-282, 298, 432, 513).

Consequently, Catholics were the targets of discrimination and their religion was the subject of public ridicule. Those in Ulster who lived in close proximity to large Protestant communities were overawed and dominated by the vigilantism and marching activities of the Orange Order and organised loyalism. Nevertheless, conservative Protestants failed to arrest the Catholic advance even in Ulster. In fact, in urban areas, like Belfast, Catholic numbers had dramatically increased since the Famine of the 1840s. There, and elsewhere, Catholics were violently opposing loyalist attempts to dominate them, and overall the infrastructure of the Catholic church was becoming more visible everywhere (Wright 1996: 10, 182-184, 241-243, 254-257, 376, 399, 417).

Growing concern about Catholic political mobilisation brought liberal and conservative Protestants closer together in a protective pan-Protestant alliance. Complete polarisation was reached in Ulster when, in the last decades of the 19th century, the Catholic reaction to organised loyalist provocation became so violent that the whole Protestant community came to identify with the fears of conservative Protestants.   In response, alienated Ulster Catholics became enthusiastic supporters of Home Rule (Wright 1996: 269-274, 372-377, 385-387-433, 502, 519-521).

The process of polarisation had a major impact on the Irish language. Up until 1850, Belfast Protestants had no difficulty accepting the Irish language as a normal part of the cultural life of the city. But as polarisation continued, the areas where Irish speakers were concentrated became Catholic, and so did the language by association. After 1860, Protestants generally were no longer prepared to show public solidarity with Irish, because it was Catholic and, therefore, suspect. Once again, the language had become politicised. From then on, the Protestants who remained interested in Irish were not representative of their community (Ó Buachalla 1968: 270-72).

During the 1840s, when the number of Irish speakers was being decimated by the Great Famine, the process of rehabilitating the language as part of the Catholic nation began within the political sphere. Thomas Davis (a Protestant) and the Young Ireland movement, influenced by German romantic nationalism, rejected Daniel O'Connell's utilitarian political philosophy. What concerned Davis was the harm that English industrial civilisation was doing to Irish nationality. He saw Irish nationality as essentially spiritual, cultivating piety, hospitality, family ties, poetry, music and learning – an organic growth, multi-confessional and multi-racial in character, but Irish (Hutchinson 1987: 98; MacDonagh 1983: 110). Attacking it, in his view, were the utilitarian, materialistic values of British liberal democracy, which would lead to moral decay, neobarbarism and ultimate collapse. The solution, he believed, was to return the Irish nation to its former greatness through the cultivation of the special qualities of Irish nationality by a united people, Catholic and Protestant. Amongst these qualities was the Irish language, which he saw as a sure barrier to anglicisation (Hutchinson 1987: 97-101). These views, together with stories and ballads romanticising the Irish past, were published in *The Nation*, a widely read weekly journal produced by Young Ireland.

The Society for the Preservation of the Irish Language

In 1876, the founding of the Society for the Preservation of the Irish Language (SPIL) brought the first group of modern revivalists together. The aim of the society was to preserve and extend the use of Irish as a spoken language (Ní Mhuiríosa 1968: 2). As a ginger group, it was very successful. It harnessed the goodwill of politicians, clergy and other influential people in campaigns to introduce the language as a subject into the school curriculum (Ní Mhuiríosa 1968: 7-10). By this stage the language was becoming identified with political nationalism.

During 1879, a split developed in SPIL. The activists, frustrated by the attitude and obstructionism of the antiquarian wing of the society, left and founded the Gaelic Union the following year. The Gaelic Union produced the first issue of its bilingual *Gaelic Journal* (*Irisleabhar na Gaedhilge*) in November 1882 (Ní Mhuiríosa 1968: 23). According to Hyde, its publication marked the beginning of the revival and cultivation of the modern language (Ní Mhuiríosa 1968: 24).

By the 1880s, cultural hostility towards England had emerged. It had two sources: the separatist movement (led by the Irish Republican Brotherhood), and the Catholic church. The former, which had its roots in Young Ireland (Hutchinson 1987: 115), saw cultural difference as a weapon in the struggle for political independence. The latter, anxious to maintain and extend its institutions (particularly in education) and confronted by anti-religious liberalism, socialism and change in Irish society (Corish 1985: 228, MacDonagh 1983: 114), was inclined to blame the religious, political and cultural ethos of the British state. Both for different reasons wanted to insulate the population from English values (Hutchinson 1987: 159).

The Gaelic Athletic Association

The Gaelic Athletic Association (GAA), which was founded for that purpose in 1884, attracted both parties immediately. The founder, Micheal Cusack, opposed the anglicisation of Irish sport as an alien, pernicious and corrupting influence (Mandle 1987: 4-5). He wanted to reverse the moral and physical degeneration of the country and create a strong autonomous Irish social life unaffected by English values through the cultivation of Irish national games (Hutchinson 1987: 158-9). Archbishop Croke, one of the GAA's patrons, who shared Cusack's views, described English literature as vicious and considered English accents, manners and entertainments alien (Mac Donagh 1983: 114).

The influence of the Irish Republican Brotherhood (IRB), grew within the GAA, a largely Catholic organisation, until by the late 1880s it controlled its communalist, parish-based structures (Mandle 1987: 64-69; Hutchinson 1987: 159). This development provoked almost nationwide opposition from the clerical wing. It was not until 1901 that antagonisms surrounding the GAA were resolved, and it emerged as a nationalist sports organisation supported by the clergy but under IRB control (Mandle 1987: 129-132).

Catholic church interest in the Irish language continued to develop in the late 1880s. A fellowship in Irish language and literature was established at University College, Dublin in 1889 (Morrissey 1983: 150) and, two years later, Fr. Eugene Growney was appointed Professor of Irish at Maynooth (Ó Tuathaigh 1995: 22-23). He was already known as an ardent language revivalist with a Catholic agenda. In 1890, he had criticised the Catholic elite for their neglect of the Irish language and its literature (which he described as the most Catholic in the world) (Growney 1890: 983). Growney began the language revival movement in Maynooth (Ó Tuathaigh 1995: 23).

A year later Eoin Mac Neill, one of the future leaders of the revival, pleaded with the Catholic clergy to promote the language. He argued that they should support the language on moral grounds because the clergy, in the past, had made it the vehicle of Christian ideas; because they had written much of the literature and were still linked by it to Ireland's Christian past; and because, in their hands, the Irish literature of the future would, unlike English and other literatures, be free from irreligion and immorality (Mac Neill 1891: 1102, 1104).

Mac Neill also warned that Ireland might cease to be a missionary nation if its national character had no other defence except religion (Mac Neill 1891: 1103).

In November the following year, Douglas Hyde, another future leader of the revival, gave his historic address on the necessity for de-anglicising Ireland. In it, he highlighted the anomalous position of the Irish who neglect everything that is Irish in their haste to adopt indiscriminately everything that is English, but who profess to hate the very country they imitate. According to him, the Irish were throwing away their best claim to a separate nationality through anglicisation but could not take the final step and become English. He believed that, in their current anomalous position, the Irish could not create worthwhile institutions or produce anything of literary or artistic value (Storey 1988: 78-80). The solution, in his opinion, was to cultivate the Irish language and everything Irish, including Anglo-Irish literature and to oppose West-Britonism.

The Gaelic League

The Gaelic League was founded on 31 July 1893. The aim of its leaders was not to create the illusion of a new Irish identity by replacing one set of social rituals with another. It was to graft dynamically on to the people the remnants of native Irish civilisation (which they considered to be the source of authentic Irish nationality) and thus create a new Gaelic Irish civilisation which would be the synthesis of tradition and modernity. They believed that what remained of native Irish civilisation was to be found preserved in the language, customs and values of contemporary rural Irish-speaking society, and that from them a new nation could be built, spiritual, artistic, peace-loving, scholarly, communalist and Christian – the antithesis of its English counterpart (Hutchinson 1987: 119-126). The creation of an Irish-speaking Ireland was therefore central to the whole endeavour. The efforts of the Gaelic League were concentrated on a number of strategies: revitalising community life in Irish-speaking (Gaeltacht) areas; creating resources and institutions for Irish speakers; teaching the language and the revivalist message to non-Irish speakers; and campaigning for linguistic rights. The work was both educational and political. Its object was to change people's attitudes, make them Irish speakers and reawaken in them, what Pearse called, the Gaelic mind (Ó Súilleabháin 1981: 164).

The compatibility of the revival with Catholic values made the Gaelic League attractive to a broad section of the Catholic clergy. The notion that Irish was a Catholic language and that English was a moral pollutant associated with Protestantism and even paganism had been gathering momentum for some time (Garvin 1986: 75). The church feared that Irish Catholic values - and the Catholic community itself - might be subverted by modern influences, particularly by the influx of unwholesome English literature, which Cardinal Logue described in 1899 as a broad and foetid stream of corruption (Coolahan 1974: 229). Clerical supporters of the league were quick to see the revival as a possible antidote. A number expressed the view that Irish should be used as a protective barrier against foreign English influences (O'Leary 1994: 20, 33). The clergy at the centre of traditional patriarchal rural Irish society were ideally placed to defend Catholic values through the promotion of the language as a community defence mechanism. As more and more clergy became involved in the movement, revivalism and the advocacy of de-anglicisation began to take on a Catholic complexion. The clergy encouraged Gaelic League and GAA activities to strengthen local Catholic communities (Hutchinson 1987: 288) and attacked English values as inimical to Catholicism as much as to Gaelic Ireland.

A key figure in the transformation of the language revival campaign into a general Catholic Irish-Ireland movement in opposition to British Protestant hegemony in Ireland was D.P. Moran, the editor of *The Leader*. He paved the way for the creation of an explicitly Gaelic Catholic identity (Hutchinson 1987: 173-174). He maintained that there were two civilisations at war in Ireland: one Gaelic, wholly Catholic and anti-English and the other, English, London-oriented and centred on the Protestant community. He argued that, if Gaelic civilisation was to prevail, nationalists would have to make an uncompromising return to core Gaelic values, rebuild Catholic social and religious life, and infuse Irish values into every sector of society (Hutchinson 1987: 175-176).

The combined crusades of the Gaelic League, the Catholic clergy, Moran's *Leader*, the GAA and others against the evils of anglicisation created an anti-British counter culture which had mass appeal. By idealising the values of Gaelic, Catholic, rural society and exploiting historic native Catholic antagonism towards the institutions and ethos of the British Protestant state it mobilised a broad constituency whose political consciousness was shaped by an ethnic Catholic communalist tradition, and offered them a 'native' Gaelic Catholic status system as an alternative to the alien British one (Hutchinson 1987: 214-215; Garvin 1987: 55).

Catholic Communalism

This Catholic communalist Gaelic counter-culture created a climate of opinion which was sympathetic to separatism, hostile towards the Protestant unionist ascendancy and suspicious of nationalists who exploited British institutions. The internal politics of the Gaelic League were affected. There were three factions, clerical, separatist and nationalist, jockeying for position. Members close to the IRB and the new Sinn Féin separatist party looked on the leadership of the organisation as Redmondites and were unhappy that they engaged in negotiations with the British authorities about concessions for Irish instead of confrontation (Ó Huallacháin 1994: 62-63). From 1907 onwards, they promoted a growing antipathy within the League towards parliamentary nationalists which was eventually reciprocated. However some nationalist MPs, like Tom O'Donnell, continued to support the League at least until 1912 (Gaughan 1983: 45-46, 97). By then, the take-over of the organisation by the IRB was well under way (Garvin 1987: 59, Ó Huallacháin 1994: 62-63).

Symptoms of political change within the Gaelic League could also be detected in Belfast. Coláiste Chomhghaill, having been established in 1905, had only been in existence for a few years when relationships between it and the Belfast Gaelic League Coiste Ceantair (District Committee) began to sour. The causes were linguistic, political and class related. The college favoured Munster Irish, which dominated Belfast at the time. Its management committee represented the older generation of Gaelic Leaguers who tended to be comfortably off middle-class Home Rulers with a romantic interest in ancient Ireland. By 1907, the dialect, programme and political values of Coláiste Chomhghaill were becoming unacceptable as Ulster provincialism grew and the Gaelic League generally became increasingly radicalised by a Catholic communalist political consciousness. From 1908 onwards, the college was being pressurised to adopt Ulster Irish. Belfast Coiste Ceantair also sought repeatedly to gain control of the college, but was continually thwarted by its management committee. Eventually, antagonism reached such a pitch that, in September 1911, Belfast Coiste Ceantair set up Ardscoil Ultach as its own Irish college in opposition to Coláiste Chomhghaill (Mac Giolla Domhnaigh 1995: 200-203).

By this stage, the fortunes of the Gaelic League were in decline. The number of its branches had fallen from 964 in 1905-6 to 262 in 1914-15 (Ó Huallacháin 1994: 72). Although it had antagonised elements within the Catholic church and lost some good friends in the Nationalist party (like Tom O'Donnell) (Gaughan 1983: 97), its decline owed more perhaps to the realisation that involvement in the Home Rule campaign might achieve more for the language in the long term than involvement in the Gaelic League (Hutchinson 1987: 293-294). According to Hutchinson (1987: 307) Gaelic revivalism was nearly moribund in 1914.

Within the Gaelic League separatist concerns continued to grow about the closeness of the moderate leadership of the organisation to parliamentary nationalism. Hyde was targeted and rumours spread that he was not really a nationalist but some kind of pro-Union imperialist (Ó Huallacháin 1994: 63-65). With the outbreak of war and the resultant polarisation within the nationalist community the IRB decided to take complete control of the Gaelic League. It arranged to have the League's 1915 Ard-Fheis packed with IRB sympathisers and a resolution was drafted to add a political dimension to the aims of the organisation (Ó Huallacháin 1994: 67-69). The upshot was that its constitution was amended to include a reference to a free Ireland; the newly elected executive had a large republican majority and Hyde resigned as president to be replaced by Mac Neill (Ó Huallacháin 1994: 69-71; Ó Broin 1985: 72-73). From this time on, according to Ó Broin, the Gaelic League was handed over root and branch to Sinn Féin, and the next three general secretaries of the organisation were either members of the IRB or the IRA (Ó Broin 1985: 72-73).

The fact that the leadership of the 1916 Rising and many of the participants had strong connections with both the Gaelic League and the GAA (Mandle 1987: 178-180; Ó Fearaíl 1975: 44, Ó Súilleabháin 1993: 15) linked both organisations in the public mind with militant nationalism. For those whose nationalist sympathies were mobilised by the Rising, both the Gaelic League and the GAA provided an outlet and a political direction. Simultaneously, and for the same reasons, they attracted the unwelcome attentions of the authorities.

From 1916 onwards, the harassment, arrest and imprisonment of Gaelic League officials, organisers and travelling teachers became common (Ó

Súilleabháin 1990: 80-82; Ó Cearúil 1995: 89-92, 94-97). Some, including senior members of the executive, used the League as cover for Sinn Féin, IRB and Volunteer activity and all were under suspicion (Ó Huallacháin 1994: 72-73; Ó Broin 1976: 175, 189; Ó Súilleabháin 1990: 88). During 1917, both the GAA and the Gaelic League, following the national trend, moved closer to Sinn Féin and the Volunteers. Before the end of the year, British intelligence was convinced that, in some counties, the GAA and Gaelic League had merged with the Sinn Féin movement (Mandle 1987: 182). By April 1918. British policy was encouraging the trend. The threat of conscription brought all these organisations closer together in united opposition (Mandle 1987: 183). Over the period 1916 to 1918 the number of Gaelic League branches rose from 312 to 551 and peaked at 700 in 1920 (Ó Fearaíl 1975: 44-45).

The gulf between both Belfast Irish colleges continued to widen in the aftermath of 1916. By then, the dialect difference was minimal, but Coláiste Chomhghaill remained associated with mild nationalism and Catholic middle class respectability, while the Coiste Ceantair and Ardscoil Ultach identified with, and were swept along by, the politics of Sinn Féin. Fr. Robert Fullerton, then curate of St. Paul's parish and a prominent and outspoken member of the party, was the chairman of the Coiste Ceantair and senior figure on the Ardscoil management committee (Mac Con Midhe 1962).

The scant use of Irish in Dáil Éireann underlined the successes and failures of the language revival. Gaelic League classes had produced a small number of fluent speakers of Irish and had given a great many others a superficial knowledge of language. The same was true of the Gaelic League's message. A small minority had come to believe that the survival and well-being of the Irish nation depended on the restoration of Irish as the language of everyday use in the community. They had found expression for their views in *An Fáinne*, an organisation for Irish speakers, established early in 1916 (Ní Murchadha 1986: 87). The majority were sympathetic to the concept of an Irish-speaking Ireland but had interpreted the Gaelic League message in relation to its ability to fulfil their own needs. In this regard, they were influenced by the way the language had been presented to them over the previous decades.

Catholic nationalists were not aware that their concept of Irishness was incomplete until they experienced the combined crusades of the Gaelic League, the Catholic church and others against the evils of anglicisation. To be truly Irish, according to the Gaelic League, it was necessary to speak Irish. However there already existed a halfway house to the Gaelic League position. It was the use of Irish as a token or symbol of ethnic distinctiveness rather than as a means of communication. This emblematic use of Irish, which had already featured in Irish nationalism at the turn of the century, flourished as the revival gathered momentum (Ó Huallacháin 1994: 57).

It involved a number of strategies to indicate that a person or institution had an Irish identity. For example an institution might adopt an Irish-language title, like Sinn Féin, or a person might begin a speech with a few words of Irish, use the Irish version of his name and address, or have signs erected in Irish. People might also feel obliged to demonstrate their Irishness by ensuring that their children studied the language at school. Similarly politicians might back language issues publicly to show solidarity with their community. In these circumstances it was possible to remain anglicised yet identify with Gaelicism and support Gaelic League campaigns for linguistic rights. Some of these campaigns themselves were instrumental in strengthening the use of Irish as an ethnic symbol (e.g., on postal addresses), without having much effect on the spread of Irish as a means of communication (Ó Huallacháin 1994: 58-60).

What the Gaelic League had succeeded in doing through its various campaigns was to provide those of the Catholic communalist tradition who had been mobilised by the Irish-Ireland movement with a badge of distinctiveness, which, like the emblems of loyalism, could be manipulated to test not only the commitment of government to the values of the community which it symbolised, but also the commitment of individuals and groups within the community itself. Invariably government reaction proved that it was anti-Irish, but even influential power blocs within nationalism were forced to pay homage as the campaign to make matriculation in Irish compulsory at the new National University illustrated. Nevertheless, as Pádraig Ó Conaire pointed out, the language was like a suit or ornament (Denvir 1978: 170-171). Beneath the veneer of Irish, Ireland the core identity for most Irish people continued to be anglicised Catholicism (Hutchinson 1987: 308).

Later, particularly after the proscription of the Gaelic League in July 1918, the emblematic role of Irish was extended to include its use as a badge of resistance. Some people, when asked by the authorities to identify themselves, ran the risk of arrest or internment by refusing to give their names except in the Irish form (Ó Huallacháin 1994: 75). This encouraged the police and military to target the language in circumstances where the emblematic usage might not have been politically motivated, like shop signs, thus intensifying its association with one specific political allegiance. Nevertheless, it was possible within Gaelic League circles to maintain that the Irish language was above politics. Although this position may have appeared dishonest to unionists, it can be explained within the narrowest context of nationalist and separatist ideology. The language was seen by some as a non-political issue *within the Irish nation,* but as a common bulwark against England (Ó Huallacháin 1994: 67).

In the autumn of 1921, morale was high amongst Belfast Gaelic Leaguers. Classes in Ardscoil Ultach and Coláiste Chomhghaill were still attracting large numbers despite the constant threat of loyalist violence. From October 1921 till March 1922, there was some semblance of Gaelic League activity in urban areas like Belfast, Derry, Armagh and Portadown, where large nationalist communities still had reasonable access to amenities for social functions. Mac Eacháin, the Gaelic League organiser for Ulster, mentioned the existence of one or two strong branches in some of these areas and a few scattered elsewhere, but, overall, his report for 1922 describes the disintegration of the Gaelic League in Northern Ireland, a process that gathered momentum as the year progressed (*Leabhrán na hArd-Fheise 1922*: 26-28). The last public function organised by the Gaelic League in Belfast was probably the St. Patrick's Day Céilí in St. Mary's Hall on 17th March.

The process of disintegration affecting the Gaelic League as an organisation had begun before 1922. As Ó Ciosáin points out, republicans, having used many Gaelic League branches as fronts for military purposes, had abandoned them as soon as subterfuge was no longer necessary following the Truce in 1921 (Ó Ciosáin 1993: 18). Other factors helped complete the process in Northern Ireland the following year. The first of these was internment which began on a large scale at the end of May, continuing on till December (Phoenix 1994: 223). Ó Ceallaigh's evidence suggests that Gaelic League activists with strong republican associations were targeted (Ó Ceallaigh 1968: 113).

Apart from internment, another major contributor to the disintegration of both the Gaelic League and the GAA was the despondency, dejection and disillusionment that swept northern nationalists on the outbreak of the civil war in June 1922, and which intensified with the death of Collins and the change in southern policy towards the north under Cosgrave, leading to feelings of betrayal, particularly in relation to the teachers' non-recognition campaign (Mac Con Midhe 1971: 5).

According to Todd (1990: 34), the political isolation of Catholics in the new northern state had allowed the Catholic church to achieve hegemony in their community. The clergy she describes as the central intellectual and political cadre of that community, organising religious, educational, socio-cultural and, to a certain extent, political activity and transmitting the tenets of their own cultural nationalism.

Irish Clergy and their Influences

Although the Gaelic League no longer functioned as an organisation in Northern Ireland in 1923, the enthusiasm for Irish had not died completely. It still survived in primary and secondary schools where some teachers loyal to Gaelic League ideals continued to teach the subject zealously.

In many instances enthusiasm for Irish in particular schools was attributable to the efforts and encouragement of clerical school managers. These priests, having become ardent Gaelic Leaguers at Maynooth or afterwards, remained convinced that the language offered northern Catholics not only access to an undivided Gaelic Ireland but also protection against the evils of the modern world which they could easily associate with the unionist values and the British Protestant ethos of the new Northern Ireland state. These priests employed teachers similar in outlook to themselves and, in some cases, strong friendships developed. Politically they were sympathetic to Sinn Féin and were religiously conservative.

In the early 1920s, some of these teachers and priests could be found working together in a number of Irish colleges, which were all that remained of the Gaelic League in the north. These included Ardscoil Ultach, Belfast, Coláiste Bhríde, Omeath, and later Coláiste Bhríde, Ranafast. It was in these colleges that the movement to revive the organisation in Ulster began.

The architect of the revival was Fr. Lorcán Ó Muireadhaigh, a dynamic worker with a strong personality and leadership qualities. He had a scholarly interest in Ireland's past and was particularly anxious to promote the revival of Irish. He saw the language primarily as a barrier against foreign civilisation. Ó Muireadhaigh shared the deep pessimism of the Irish bishops about the moral dangers threatening the Catholic community in Ireland in the aftermath of the civil war. The bishops were particularly concerned that the traditional moral values and the nature of Irish society were being undermined by a flood of foreign influences attributable, in their view, to sensational English mass-circulation newspapers, the cinema, new styles of dress and modern dancing (Whyte 1971: 24-28). Ó Muireadhaigh went a stage further by attributing all of these evils to the impact of English civilisation on Ireland following the widespread adoption of the English language by the Irish people (Ua Muireadhaigh 1928: 8). He and other priests of his generation had come to the conclusion that the only effective way of protecting Irish society against these evils was to revive the Irish language and develop a Gaelic outlook.

A Gaelic outlook, according to Ó Muireadhaigh, was the realisation that there was a battle in process between two cultures, the ancient aristocratic Gaelic culture and a new culture which was pervading the country from the outside. He believed that the latter was easy to recognise because of the evil lifestyle associated with it, disreputable newspapers, dances, films, plays, literature, fashions and evil filthy habits of every kind. Therefore, he equated the Gaelic outlook with the promotion of the Catholic faith and claimed that most priests would not be active in the revival if they did not share his view (Ua Muireadhaigh 1928: 4). Ó Muireadhaigh's enthusiasm for the revival of Irish was motivated by his desire to protect the values of patriarchal Irish Catholic society from anglicisation and modernism. For him and his clerical associates, it was essentially a Catholic crusade. When Comhaltas Uladh was founded in November 1926, twelve of the twenty-strong executive were priests.

The re-organising of the Gaelic League in Northern Ireland which followed had begun to attract the attention of the police by September 1927. The RUC informed the Ministry of Home Affairs that a public meeting under the auspices of the Gaelic League would be held in St. Paul's Hall, Hawthorn Street, Belfast, on 5 October; that it would be chaired by Dr. MacRory, and addressed by Lord Ashbourne, a prominent Gaelic Leaguer. The purpose of this meeting, they believed, was to generate enthusiasm within the language movement for the winter session and that similar meetings had been held annually before the unrest. The police report of the meeting itself mentioned that there was a large attendance and that "The local suspects and a large number of past and present members of the IRA were present" (PRONI HA 36/1/366). The meeting may have had a strong republican presence, but the fact that Devlinite clergy were there, and that Devlin himself apologised for being absent because of another engagement, indicated that there was also support for the language amongst parliamentary nationalists. Of greater significance to unionists, undoubtedly, was the location, and the presence of Mac Rory and seven priests on the platform, identifying the event completely with Catholicism ("The Irish language", *The Irish News*, 8 October 1927).

Before proposing a vote of thanks to the speakers Fr. Fullerton told the crowd that he was going to see to it that the Gaels of Belfast had a hall worthy of them – a central rallying place for the social uplifting of the community; that they would have to create a new atmosphere and get back, if possible, to Irish life such as it was, as it should be, and as it never should have ceased to be. Then he called on the GAA and the Gaelic League to work together. Fundraising efforts culminated in a Grand Bazaar in February 1929, which lasted six days, and the hall was opened shortly afterwards.

No sooner was the Bazaar over than there was trouble in Belfast Coiste Ceantair. Some members took great exception to what they considered was the undue respect accorded to Joseph Devlin and his political party during the week's events. The truth was that Devlin had made a very generous donation to the Bazaar and the organising committee felt that they had little alternative but to invite him to attend a number of functions. However, nothing would satisfy the malcontents who needed a scapegoat. They found one in the shape of Seán Mac Maoláin, who was secretary of Belfast Coiste Ceantair, and who, as secretary of the organising committee of the Bazaar, was responsible for inviting Devlin to attend the event.

According to Mac Maoláin (1969: 155-159), those who were making life difficult for him were fearful that Devlin's involvement in the Bazaar would encourage the Devlinites to attempt a take-over of the Gaelic League in Belfast. The Devlinites were quite capable of doing so at any time, if they had wanted, as Mac Maoláin points out, because they were the strongest nationalist grouping in the city. However, the fact that they did not was of no consolation to Mac Maoláin who eventually decided not only to resign from the Coiste Ceantair but also to migrate to Dublin where he found employment as a translator with An Gúm, the state-funded publishing scheme for books in Irish.

It is clear from the fate of such a senior Gaelic League figure as Mac Maoláin that powerful political forces were at play within the organisation, despite protestations to the contrary. Superficially, it seems as though Mac Maoláin was a victim of republican antipathy towards Devlinism and that the organisation, at least in Belfast, was dominated by republicans. In fact, the situation was slightly more complicated. Mac Maoláin was not a Devlinite. Politically, he was close to republicanism and was on good terms with influential figures, such as Fr. Fullerton and Ó Muireadhaigh, who were well regarded by republicans. If Mac Maoláin's future had depended on his standing amongst republicans alone, judging by his friends, there is good reason to believe that he might not have felt compelled to resign. The fact that he did suggests that he was experiencing hostility from a much broader constituency which could be mobilised in opposition to Devlinism, and which was, arguably, the real political force behind the Gaelic League and the Irish Ireland movement – that is, Catholic communalism.

Irish-Language Communalism

However, there were already signs that another ideology was growing within the Gaelic League in the North. The first of these signs was to be found in a concern about the definition of the words 'Gael' and 'Gaelicism'. Depending on the speaker, they could mean either 'Irish Irelander' and 'Irish-Ireland mentality', or 'Irish speaker' and 'Irish-speaking mentality'. The different usage reflected the existence of two different constituencies within the Gaelic League and there was evidence of some friction between them.

The majority, who belonged to the anglicised Catholic communalist tradition, valued the language as an important badge of distinctiveness, but it was not central to their lives. They were prepared to learn enough Irish to satisfy their needs, but they reserved their enthusiasm for Gaelic games and Irish dancing. The minority, who were committed to the creation of an Irish-speaking Ireland, were already becoming critical of them. In November 1935, Fr. McGuckian, president of Feis na nGleann, spoke disparagingly of those associated with Gaelic games and Irish dancing, who called themselves 'Gaels' though they did not know a word of Irish ("Feis na nGleann Committee", *The Irish News*, 14 November 1935). Some months later Basil Mac Uilis, secretary of Gaedheal Uladh argued that although Gaelicism included the promotion of Irish dancing and Irish games, it was defined primarily by one's ability to speak Irish. What concerned him was that most of those involved in Gaedheal Uladh neglected the language in favour of dancing and games (Mac Uilis 1936: 23-24).

The debate about the nature of Gaelicism amongst Irish speakers was complemented by efforts to make the language more relevant to their lives. In 1934, Belfast Coiste Ceantair began conducting its affairs completely through the medium of Irish and, a year later, Craobh Thír na nÓg established An Cumann Gaelach, a social club for Irish speakers in the city. Other factors shaped developments in the 1940s. There was the influence of *Glúin na Buaidhe* (Mac an Bheatha 1967: 165, 180), the Gaelicisation of numerous republicans who had learned to speak Irish while interned during the Second World War (Ó hUid 1985: 137-140), the establishment of *An Réalt* in October 1949, and the emergence of Cumann Chluain Ard as one of the most dynamic Gaelic League branches in Belfast (Mag Aonghusa 1945: 22-27). The net result was that, by the early 1950s, a small circle of Irish-speaking intellectuals existed within the city. Inspired by the writings of Seosamh Mac Grianna, they sought to construct a set of values and an institutional framework that would bring a modern independent Irish-speaking society into existence, using what remained intact and worthwhile of pre-colonial Gaelic Ireland. They emphasised the preservation and development of the Gaeltacht and the establishment locally of a variety of Irish-speaking institutions in the belief that they might coalesce eventually, creating the nucleus of this new society. Furthermore, they insisted that, at all times and in all activities, only Irish should be used. To do otherwise, they believed, would undermine the objective ("Tuairisc na Cathrach", *An tUltach*, 29 (12), 1952: 7; "An Béarla, cuidiú nó bac?", *Dearcadh*, 1 (3), Márta, 1954: 4-6).

This new ideology, Irish-language communalism, which was articulated by the organisation *Fál*, became the main preoccupation of Cumann Chluain Ard ("Tuairisc na Cathrach", *An tUltach*, 30 (1), 1953: 9). This Gaelic League branch was used as a base for attempts to create and expand a range of activities that would form an integral part of the normal life of a modern urban Irish-speaking society. The most successful of these was the establishment, in 1969, of an Irish-speaking community in a small housing development in West Belfast, followed by the founding of an Irish-medium primary school there in 1971. This has opened up a new and exciting chapter in the history of the language in Northern Ireland which continues to unfold.

Although there is currently unprecedented optimism about the future of the Irish language in Northern Ireland, it may be misplaced. There is strong evidence to suggest that, since the 1980s, following the rise of Sinn Féin, Catholic communalism has once again replaced Irish-language communalism as the dominant ideology within the Irish language movement. If this is true, the repercussions of such a development could signal the end of the current phase of the Irish language revival in Northern Ireland, but that is a story for another day.

Acknowledgement

The author would like to thank to the Deputy Keeper of the Records, The Public Record Office of Northern Ireland, for permission to quote from PRONI sources.

References

Barnard, T. C., 1993, "Protestants and the Irish Language, c. 1675-1725", *Journal of Ecclesiastical History*, 44 (2)

Bartlett, T., 1992, *The Fall and Rise of the Irish Nation: The Catholic Question 1690-1830*, Dublin: Gill and Macmillan

Clarke, A., 1978, "Colonial identity in early seventeenth-century Ireland", in Moody, T.W., ed., *Nationality and the Pursuit of National Independence; Papers read before the Irish Conference of Historians: Historical Studies vol XI*

Connolly, S. J., 1982, *Priests and People in Pre-Famine Ireland*, Dublin: Gill and Macmillan

Connolly, S. J., 1989a, "The Catholic question, 1801-12", in Vaughan, W.E., ed., *A New History of Ireland V: Ireland under the Union I, 1800-1870*, Oxford: Clarendon Press

Connolly, S. J., 1989b, "Mass politics and sectarian conflict, 1823-30", in Vaughan, W.E., ed., *A New History of Ireland V: Ireland under the Union I, 1800-1870*, Oxford: Clarendon Press

Corish, P. J., 1985, *The Irish Catholic Experience: A Historical Survey*, Dublin : Gill and Macmillan

Cullen, L. M., 1990, "Patrons, teachers and literacy in Irish, 1700-1850", in Daly, M., et al., eds., *The Origins of Popular Literacy in Ireland: Language Change and Educational Development, 1700-1920*, Dublin: Department of Modern History TCD and Department of Modern History UCD

Cunningham, B., 1986, "Native culture and political change in Ireland, 1580-1640", in Brady, C. and Gillespie, R., eds., *Natives and Newcomers: Essays on the making of Irish Colonial Society 1534-1641*, Dublin: Irish Academic Press

Cunningham, B., 1989, "The culture and ideology of the Irish Franciscans at Louvain 1607-1650", in Brady, C., ed., *Ideology and the Historians: Papers read before the Irish Conference of Historians held at Trinity College, Dublin, 8-10 June 1989, Historical Studies XVII*

De Brún, P., 1983, "The Irish Society's bible teachers", *Éigse*, XIX

Denvir, G., ed., 1978, *Aistí Phádraic Uí Chonaire*, Inveran: Cló Chois Fharraige

Durkacz, V. E., 1983, *The Decline of the Celtic Languages*, Edinburgh: John Donald

Garvin, T., 1986, "Priests and patriots: Irish separatism and fear of the modern 1890-1914", *Irish Historical Studies*, XXV (97)

Garvin, T., 1987, "The politics of language and literature in pre-independence Ireland", *Irish Political Studies*, 2

Gaughan, J. A., 1983, *A Political Oddessy: Thomas O'Donnell*, Dublin: Kingdom Books

Growney, E., 1890, "The national language", *Irish Ecclesiastical Record*, 3rd series, XI (11)

Harrison, A., 1988, *Ag Cruinniú Meala: Anthony Raymond (1675-1726), Ministéir Protastúnach, agus Léann na Gaeilge i mBaile Átha Cliath*, Dublin: An Clóchomhar

Hutchinson, J., 1987, *The Dynamics of Cultural Nationalism: the Gaelic Revival and the Creation of the Irish Nation State*, London: Allen and Unwin

Inglis, T., 1987, *Moral Monopoly: The Catholic Church in Modern Irish Society*, Dublin: Gill and Macmillan

Inglis, T., 1991, "The struggle for control of the Irish body: state, church, and society in nineteenth century Ireland", in Wolf, E.R., ed., *Religion, Regimes and State-Formation: Perspectives from European Ethnology*, New York: State University of New York Press

Leerssen, J. Th., 1986, *Mere Irish and Fíor-Ghael: Studies in the Idea of Irish Nationality, its Development and Literary Expression prior to the Nineteenth Century*, Amsterdam: John Benjamins

Mac an Bheatha, P., 1967, *Téid Focal le Gaoith*, Dublin: FNT

Mac Con Midhe, P., 1962, "Father Bob Fullerton", *The Irish News*, 13, 14 December

Mac Con Midhe, P., 1971, "Stair na Gaeilge i scoileanna na sé gcontae (1)", *An tUltach*, 48 (5)

MacDonagh, O., 1983, *States of Mind: a Study of Anglo-Irish Conflict 1780-1980*, London: George Allen and Unwin

Mac Giolla Domhnaigh, G., 1995, *Conradh na Gaeilge Chúige Uladh ag Tús an 20ú Chéid*, Belfast: Comhaltas Uladh de Chonradh na Gaeilge

MacMahon, J. A., 1981, "The Catholic clergy and the social question in Ireland, 1891-1916", *Studies*, Winter

Mac Maoláin, S., 1969, *Gleann Airbh go Glas Naíon*, Dublin: Government Publications

Mac Neill, J., 1891, "Why and how the Irish language is to be preserved", *Irish Ecclesiastical Record*, 3rd series, XII

Mac Uilis, B. C., 1936, "Craobh Ghaedheal Uladh", in *Gaedhil Uladh*, Belfast: Craobh Ghaedheal Uladh

Mag Aonghusa, S., 1945, "Cumann Chluain Ard: its history, its purpose", *Thomas Davis Centenary Week*, Belfast: Cumann Chluain Ard

Mandle, W. F., 1987, *The Gaelic Athletic Association and Irish Nationalist Politics 1884-1924*, Dublin: Gill and Macmillan

Morrissey, T. J., 1983, *Towards a National University: William Delany SJ (1835-1924): An Era of Initiative in Irish education*, Dublin: Wolfhound Press

Ní Mhuiríosa, M., 1968, *Réamhchonraitheoirí*, Dublin: Clódhanna Teoranta

Ó Broin, L., 1978, *Revolutionary Underground: The Story of the Irish Republican Brotherhood 1858-1924*, Dublin: Gill and Macmillan

Ó Broin, L., 1985, *Protestant Nationalists in Revolutionary Ireland: The Stopford Connection*, Dublin: Gill and Macmillan

Ó Buachalla, B., 1968, *I mBéal Feirste Cois Cuain*, Dublin: An Clóchomhar

Ó Buachalla, B., 1983, "Na Stíobhartaigh agus an t-aos léinn: Cing Séamus", *Proceedings of the Royal Irish Academy*, 83c

Ó Buachalla, B., 1993, "James our true king: the ideology of Irish royalism in the seventeenth century", in Boyce, D.G. et al., eds., *Political Thought in Ireland since the Seventeenth Century*, London: Routledge

Ó Ceallaigh, E., 1968, *An Dá Thaobh*, Dublin: An Clóchomhar

Ó Cearúil, C., 1995, *Aspail ar son na Gaeilge: Timirí na Gaeilge 1899-1923*, Dublin: Conradh na Gaeilge

Ó Ciosáin, E., 1993, *An t-Éireannach 1934-1937: Páipéar Sóisialach Gaeltachta*, Dublin: An Clóchomhar

Ó Ciosáin, N., 1997, *Print and Popular Culture in Ireland, 1750-1850*, London: Macmillan Press

Ó Conchúir, B., 1982, *Scríobhaithe Chorcaí 1700-1850*, Dublin: An Clóchomhar

Ó Cuív, B., 1986, "Irish language and literature 1691-1845" in, Moody, T.W. et al., eds., *A New History of Ireland IV: Eighteenth Century Ireland 1691-1800*, Oxford: Clarendon Press

Ó Fearaíl, P., 1975, *The Story of Conradh na Gaeilge*, Dublin: Clódhanna Teoranta

Ó Háinle, C., 1994, "Ó chaint na ndaoine go dtí an caighdeán oifigiúil", in Mc Cone et al., eds., *Stair na Gaeilge*, Maynooth: Roinn na Sean-Ghaeilge

Ó Huallacháin, C., 1994, *The Irish and Irish: A Sociolingual Analysis of the Relationship between a People and their Language*, Dublin: Irish Franciscan Provincial Office

Ó hUid, T., 1985, *Faoi Ghlas*, Westport: FNT

O'Leary, P., 1994, *The Prose Literature of the Gaelic Revival, 1881-1921: Ideology and Innovation*, Pennsylvania: The Pennsylvania State University Press

Ó Súilleabháin, D., 1981, *An Piarsach agus Conradh na Gaeilge*, Dublin Clódhanna Teoranta

Ó Súilleabháin, D., 1990, *Na Timirí i Ré Thosaigh an Chonartha 1899-1927*, Dublin: Conradh na Gaeilge

Ó Súilleabháin, D., 1993, "Conradh na Gaeilge agus an t-éirí amach", *Feasta*, XLVI (4) Aibreán

Ó Tuathaigh, G., 1995, "Maigh Nuad agus stair na Gaeilge", in Ó Síocháin, E., ed., *Maigh Nuad: Saothrú na Gaeilge 1795-1995*, Maynooth: An Sagart

Ó Tuathaigh, M. A. G., 1986, "An chléir Chaitliceach, an léann dúchais agus an cultúr in Éirinn c.1750 – c.1850" in *Léann na Cléire: Léachtaí Cholm Cille XVI*

Phoenix, E., 1994, *Northern Nationalism: Nationalist Politics, Partition and the Catholic Minority in Northern Ireland 1890-1940*, Belfast: Ulster Historical Foundation

Storey, M., ed., 1988, *Poetry and Ireland since 1800: a Source Book*, London: Routledge

Todd, J., 1990, "Northern Irish nationalist political culture", *Irish Political Studies*, 5

Ua Muireadhaigh, L.P., 1928, "An troid in aghaidh na ndroch-dhamhsaí agus na ndroch-pháipéirí", *An tUltach*, 5 (6)

Whyte, J. H., 1974, *Church and State in Modern Ireland, 1923-1970*, Dublin: Gill and Macmillan

Williams, N., 1986, *I bPrionta I Leabhar: na Protastúin agus Prós na Gaeilge 1567-1724*, Dublin: An Clóchomhar

Wright, F., 1996, *Two Lands on One Soil: Ulster Politics before Home Rule*, Dublin: Gill and Macmillan

Annual Reports
The Gaelic League
Leabhrán na hArd-Fheise

Dissertations
Coolahan, J. M., 1974, *A study of curricular policy for the primary and secondary schools of Ireland 1900-1935, with special reference to the Irish language and Irish history*, unpublished PhD. dissertation, Trinity College Dublin

Ní Mhurchadha, M., 1986, *Pleanáil Teanga i leith na Gaeilge 1800-1922*, unpublished PhD. Dissertation, Trinity College Dublin

Language Rights as Human Rights in Europe and in Northern Ireland

Dónall Ó Riagáin

Post World War II Europe did not offer a friendly environment to minorities, their languages, their cultures or their political aspirations. The continent had been ravaged, millions were dead and unemployed, and the polarisation between the liberal democratic world of western Europe and that of communist eastern Europe was becoming all too evident.

Memories were still very much alive of how Hitler had used the presence of German minorities outside of the Reich as an excuse for interfering in the internal affairs of other states and, in some instances (e.g. Czechoslovakia), invading them. There was also the impression, in many instances grossly exaggerated, that disgruntled minorities had collaborated with the invading Nazis (e.g. in Flanders and in Brittany), and that the best way forward for western Europe was to keep such groups firmly in check. Even if the western powers did not like Stalin or Tito, they at least offered an element of stability after which so many sought.

In 1948, the UN's Universal Declaration of Human Rights was adopted[1]. The Universal Declaration of Human Rights had nothing to say about the rights of linguistic minorities. However, Article 2 of the Declaration does contain an important reference to language:

Article 2.
> *Everyone is entitled to all the rights and freedoms set out in this Declaration, without distinction of any kind, such as race, colour, sex, language, religion, political or other opinion, national or social origin, property, birth or other status.*
> *Furthermore, no distinction shall be made on the basis of the political, jurisdictional or international status of the country or territory to which a person belongs, whether it be independent, trust, non-self-governing or under any other limitation of sovereignty.*

We see here established the principle that language cannot be used as a basis for denying the fundamental human rights, outlined in the Declaration, to any person.

Two years later, the Council of Europe adopted its Convention for the Protection of Human Rights and Fundamental Freedoms that carried an almost identical provision in Article 14.

---

[1]   Adopted by the General Assembly of the United Nations on 10 December 1948

The UN developed this concept, notably in its International Covenant on Civil and Political Rights[2].

Other UN agencies (e.g. the International Labour Organisation and UNESCO) were also active in this regard. The International Labour Organisation declared in its Convention concerning the Protection and integration of indigenous and other tribal and semi-tribal populations in independent countries[3]:

> *Article 23.*
>
> *1.   Children belonging to the populations concerned shall be taught to read and write in their mother tongue or, where this is not practicable, in the language most commonly used by the group to which they belong.*
>
> *2.   Provision shall be made for a progressive transition from the mother tongue or vernacular language to the national language or to one of the official languages of the country.*
>
> *3.   Appropriate measures shall, as far as possible, be taken to preserve the mother tongue or the vernacular language.*

Reductive bilingualism, maybe, but at least a major step forward from total non-recognition!

UNESCO in its Convention against Discrimination in Education[4] stated in Article 5:

> *1.   The state parties to this convention agree that ....*
>
> *It is essential to recognise the rights of members of national minorities to carry on their own educational activities, including the maintenance of schools and, depending on the educational policy of each state, the use of the teaching of their own language.........*

Positive developments came even slower at European level. The Council of Ministers of the European Union, or the European Communities as it was then known, recognised certain defined official and working languages. The EU, however, made no reference to, or no provision for, the regional or minority languages spoken by some millions of its citizens. It is interesting to note that, in the original European Coal and Steel Community of 1951, it was envisaged that French be the sole working language. [Indeed, the French text is the only authentic, as distinct from official, version of the Treaty]. Protests from the

---

[2]   International Covenant on Civil and Political Rights, adopted by the General Assembly of the UN on 16 December 1966 and entered into force on 23 March 1976

[3]   ILO Convention (No. 107) concerning the protection and integration of indigenous and other tribal and semi-tribal populations in independent countries, adopted 25 June 1957

[4]   Adopted on 14 December 1960 by the General Conference of the UN Educational, Scientific and Cultural Organization

Flemings, who feared that the linguistic balance of Belgium could be disturbed, resulted in Dutch, German and Italian being added. English, Danish, Greek, Spanish, Portuguese, Swedish and Finnish joined the list of official languages as the Community expanded. In addition, Irish is a 'treaty' language, i.e. there are versions of the Treaties and other basic documents in Irish which are co-official with those in the eleven official and working languages. Furthermore, Irish may be used in the European Parliament and in the Court of Justice subject to certain conditions.

The first signs of interest in the future of the Communities' regional and minority languages appeared in the European Parliament in 1979. A motion for resolution was tabled by John Hume MEP[5] and co-signed by a Socialist deputy from all the member states, calling for the drawing up of a 'Bill of Rights of the Regional Languages and Cultures of the Community'. In the event, the Parliament decided to have a report drawn up on the promotion of regional and minority languages. Gaetano Arfé, MEP, a former Professor of History in the University of Firenze and a highly respected parliamentarian, was appointed *rapporteur*. His report and Resolution[6] were adopted by the European Parliament on 16 October 1981, thus giving a political basis for Community action of favour of such languages. A further resolution, again prepared by Arfé[7] was adopted in 1983, as were resolutions from Kuijpers[8] in 1987, and Killilea[9] in 1994. The European Communities adopted a small budget line for this work in 1982 and, the following year, the European Parliament set up an Intergroup Committee for Minority Languages, which is still functioning. Encouraged by such developments, a small number of language activists, many of them Irish, established in 1982 the European Bureau for Lesser Used Languages, in an effort to speak and act for such languages at European level.

In short, an understanding of linguistic rights started to evolve. That is to say, linguistic rights as an integral part of human rights in general or at least closely related to them. But what may we regard as linguistic *rights* as distinct from the demands and aspirations of linguistic communities, especially those in a marginalized position? Before attempting a response, we must add the caveat that society's understanding of human rights in general is not set in stone, nor is it static. For instance, what today we regard unquestioningly as being the rights of women, were not regarded as such thirty of forty years ago. A reliable indicator as to what are now generally excepted as being linguistic rights can be found in two documents, prepared by the Foundation on Inter-Ethnic Relations for the OSCE High Commissioner on National Minorities: The Hague

---

[5] B3-0016/90

[6] Resolution on a Community charter of Regional Languages and Cultures and on a Charter of Ethnic Minorities, adopted by the European Parliament on 16 October 1981

[7] Resolution on Measures in favour of minority languages and cultures, adopted by the European Parliament on 11 February 1983

[8] Resolution on the Languages and Cultures of regional and Ethnic Minorities in the European Community, adopted by the European Parliament on 30 October 1987

[9] Resolution on the Linguistic and Cultural Minorities in the European Community, adopted by the European Parliament on 9 February 1994

Recommendations Regarding the Education Rights of National Minorities[10], and The Oslo Recommendations on the Linguistic Rights of National Minorities[11]. What is interesting about these two sets of recommendations is that they are not new legal or political documents but rather compilations of basic education and linguistic rights, as defined in existing legal and political documents.

The education rights include the right, not only to have the minority language taught, but also to have it used as a medium of instruction. Also included is the right of the minority to establish and manage their own private educational institutions, and it stresses that the state should not hinder the enjoyment of this right by burdensome legal and administrative requirements. Other linguistic rights include the rights of persons belonging to national minorities to have access to broadcast time in their own language on publicly funded media. They should also have the right to acquire civil documents and certificates both in the official language[s] of the state and in their own language from regional and/or local public institutions. Public services should be made available in the language of the minority. Elected members of regional or local governmental bodies should be able to use the minority language during activities relating to these bodies. They should also have the right to express themselves in their own language in judicial proceedings, if necessary with the free assistance of an interpreter and/or translator. The above rights are subject to members of the minority being present in significant numbers and their expressing the desire to use their language.

It is only in very recent times that even some of the aforementioned rights have come to be accepted in Northern Ireland.

However, the clearest and most comprehensive exposition of minority language rights can be found in the European Charter for Regional or Minority Languages[12].

The European Charter for Regional or Minority Languages is a unique document in a number of ways. It is, to the best of my knowledge, the only international convention of its kind, exclusively directed at conserving and promoting regional or minority languages. It is interesting also in that it does not seek to confer rights on minorities or ethnic groups. They are not even mentioned. Neither does it speak of linguistic communities. It is addressed at languages. But all living languages exist because people use them and, if languages are accorded rights, those who use them will also become beneficiaries.

Therefore, we should not be surprised to find the following sentence in the Preamble to the Charter:

> *Considering that the right to use a regional or minority language in private and public life is an inalienable right conforming to the principles embodied in the United Nations International Covenant on Civil and*

> Political Rights, and according to the spirit of the Council of Europe Convention for the Protection of Human Rights and Fundamental Freedoms.

Maybe it is appropriate at this juncture to add a word about the issue of terminology. Those who drafted the Charter were only too aware that terms like "regional or minority" were not perfect. But they were the most acceptable at the time. This should not cause any problems. I think we should all simply refer to Article 1 of the Charter where the terminology is explained in a clear and unambiguous manner.

It is also worthwhile noting that the Charter cannot be misused to undermine the integrity of the state. Article 5 clearly states:

> Nothing in this Charter may be interpreted as implying any right to engage in any activity or perform any action in contravention of the purposes of the Charter of the United Nations or other obligations under international law, including the principle of sovereignty and territorial integrity of States.

There are five parts in the Charter:

Part I **General Provisions**
  This deals primarily with definitions, undertakings and practical arrangements.

Part II **Objectives and Principles**
  All contracting parties [i.e. ratifying states] are obliged to accept these objectives and principles.

Part III **Measure to promote the use of regional or minority languages in public life**
  This is where we find details of the practical measures required of states in the various domains of life where language is used – Education, Judicial authorities, Administrative authorities and public services, Media, Cultural activities and facilities, Economic and social life and Transfrontier exchanges.

Part IV **Application of the Charter**
  Here we find out about the furnishing of reports and the role of the committee of experts.

Part V **Final Provisions**
  The procedure for signing, ratifying and the coming into effect of the Charter is set out here.

Part I deals with definitions. In its definition of "regional or minority languages" it excludes dialects and migrant languages. Interestingly, in Article 3 it states that the Charter can be applied, not only to regional or minority languages, but also to an "official language which is less widely used on the whole or part of the national territory". This was inserted to accommodate the position of the Irish language in Ireland, which is constitutionally the national and first official language of the state, although sadly lesser used for historical reasons. Unfortunately, the Irish Government has refused to sign the Charter on the grounds that signing might undermine the legal position of Irish. Another point worth noting is Article 4.2 which states that "the provisions of the Charter shall not affect any more favourable provisions concerning the status of regional or minority languages....."

All ratifying parties must accept the provisions of Part II and apply the objectives set out in Article 7.1 to all the languages in the state. They may, however, at the time of ratification make reservations on paragraphs 2 to 5 of this Article. Paragraph 5 refers to the application of the principles set out in paragraphs 1 to 4 *mutatis mutandis* to non-territorial languages i.e. Gypsy and Jewish languages. Croatia has made a reservation on this paragraph. Languages to be covered by Part III must be named at the time of ratification as well as the territories on which the provisions will be applied.

It is Part III that we find the substance of the Charter. There are 7 articles in this Part and each article has paragraphs and sub-paragraphs:

Article 8:	*Education*
Article 9:	*Judicial authorities*
Article 10:	*Administrative authorities and public services*
Article 11:	*Media*
Article 12:	*Cultural activities and facilities*
Article 13:	*Economic and social life*
Article 14:	*Transfrontier exchanges*

A ratifying state must apply a minimum of 35 paragraphs or sub-paragraphs from the provisions of Part III to each named language to be covered, including at least three paragraphs or sub-paragraphs from Articles 8 and 12 and a minimum of one from Articles 9, 10, 11 and 13. As can be seen, ratifying the Charter is a serious undertaking and not merely a vague expression of tolerance and good intentions. Some critics have described Part III as an *à la carte* menu. I reject this and counter by saying it is more like a *table d'hôte* one. You must chose something from each course. It is not for snacks!

It is clear from Paragraph 50 of the Explanatory Report, accompanying the Charter, that there is nothing to prevent any ratifying state from upgrading its regime of support for its regional or minority languages, by naming new languages to be covered by Part III or by choosing stronger measures to support them. The Netherlands has already done so and Germany is preparing to do the same. In the case of Northern Ireland, this provision is very important for proponents of Irish and Ulster-Scots.

The provisions for the application of the Charter, as found in Part IV, are also very interesting. Within a year of the Charter coming into effect for a state, it must supply a written report on its implementation to the Council of Europe. It must provide further reports every three years thereafter. These reports must be made public. A committee of experts examines these reports and eventually makes its own report to the Committee of Ministers. The Committee of Ministers may make this report public. Bodies or associations legally established in a ratifying state may draw the attention of the committee of experts to matters relating to the undertakings entered into by the state under Part III of the Charter. After consulting with the state, the committee may take account of this information when preparing its report. In a word, citizens may complain that a state is not meeting its obligations under the terms of its instrument of ratification. And, in turn, the committee of experts may act on this information. I can say, from what I know of the work of the committee of experts, that it is taking its responsibilities very seriously and has visited a number of states to check on the situation pertaining there.

In short, I think that the monitoring mechanism is proving to be quite effective and, all in all, the Charter is proving to be a stronger document than some of us thought it might be.

The final provisions of Part V are of a technical nature, relating to the procedure of ratifying the Charter and its coming into effect.

At the present time, nine countries have ratified the European Charter for Regional or Minority Languages and another 14 have signed it. The countries that have ratified are Norway, Finland, Hungary, the Netherlands, Germany, Switzerland, Croatia, Liechtenstein and Sweden. Austria, Cyprus, Denmark, Iceland, France, Luxembourg, Malta, Romania, Slovenia, Spain, the Former Yugoslav Republic of Macedonia, the Ukraine, Italy and the United Kingdom have signed but have not yet ratified. The Danish instrument of ratification is in preparation, being delayed only because of a demand by the Faeroese for greater autonomy. Italy, shortly after enacting domestic legislation on her regional languages, signed the Charter and is expected to ratify without any undue delay. Legislation has been introduced in the Spanish parliament to enable that country to ratify. Austria, too, is reported to be positively examining the implications of ratification. I spoke at a seminar in Moscow in May where the representative of the Ministry of Foreign Affairs promised that Russia would sign this year. Ratification is expected to take five or six years, the delay being due largely to financial difficulties. As over 130 languages are involved, one can understand the financial implications of ratifying. Russia is undoubtedly the "big one". More languages are entailed than in the case of all the ratifying states put together. Furthermore, a Russian signature should have a positive influence on other states in Eastern Europe. It is our biggest challenge to date. But succeed we will!

The then Secretary of State for Wales, Ron Davies, announced in June 1998 that the UK would sign the Charter and on ratification would apply Part III to Welsh, Scottish Gaelic and Irish in Northern Ireland. In addition, Part II would be applied to Scots. Representations were made to have Part II cover extended to Ulster-Scots, and I am glad to say that these representations did not fall on deaf ears.   On 2 March 2000, the UK signed.   In a letter sent by the UK and Irish governments to Northern Ireland political parties on 5 May, following on the restoration of the Northern Ireland Executive and Assembly, it is stated that the UK Government would ratify the Charter by September 2000 and would publish within six months an action plan to implement it.

When speaking of the Charter it is imperative to understand that a ratifying state can chose in its instrument of ratification only those provisions that are already in place.   The Charter is not an action plan for implementing a language policy.   Less still is it a political manifesto.   It is a legally binding instrument, an international Convention, which obliges a State to honour certain commitments, which it has freely undertaken.

What paragraphs and sub-paragraphs from Part III will be applied to Welsh, Scottish Gaelic and Irish?   We do not know: we will have to await the instrument of ratification.   However, we can be reasonably sure of some things. The provisions for Welsh will almost certainly be strong by virtue of the fact that such measures are already in place.   Those for Gàidhlig will be weaker, reflecting the position of that language.   And those for Irish will be weaker still for the simple reason that that language enjoys little official support in Northern Ireland. Should the Irish language movement be disappointed?   Should it dismiss the Charter as being next to useless?   Most certainly, not.   It should derive satisfaction from the fact that Irish is now the subject of an international legal instrument and enjoys a higher level of legal recognition in Northern Ireland than it did at any time since the Flight of the Earls.   Even more so, it should set about having the position of Irish enhanced, in line with the provisions of the Good Friday Belfast Agreement so that the UK instrument of ratification can be upgraded within a certain period – say three to five years.

For the speakers of Ulster-Scots the Charter is, if anything, even more significant as hitherto their speech-form has enjoyed no official recognition whatever.   They too should set about having the position of their language strengthened so that it too could be covered by Part III within a given period.

Northern Ireland is moving into a new era, and its linguistic and cultural heritage, in my opinion, may hold the key to success.   A fear of having the distinct identity of one's own community submerged or even suppressed has been at the heart of much of confrontational politics in Northern Ireland.   The reality is that both communities have been culturally impoverished – one angry and resentful because of it, the other barely aware of it happening.   The Good Friday Agreement is radical in its approach to linguistic and cultural diversity, more radical, in my opinion than the vision of Wolfe Tone who aspired to "…substitute the common name of Irishman in place of the denominations of Protestant, Catholic and Dissenter …"[13].   The Agreement, not only seeks to conserve and foster our rich linguistic diversity, but goes further in declaring it to be part of the cultural wealth of the island of Ireland.   It goes on to propose concrete steps to achieve this, especially in the case of Irish.

---

[13]   Quoted from R. Barry O'Brien, *The Autobiography of Theobald Wolfe Tone* (London, 1893)

The challenge facing us is daunting, not only because of the enormity and complexity of the tasks confronting us, but even more so because it demands of us that we think differently – indeed see each other and ourselves differently. The "leprechaun language" and the "DIY language for unionists" become our common heritage, bringing with them self-respect and pride in our identity. The cynics will say that it is impracticable, unrealistic. But then cynics do not achieve change for the better. I find the challenge exciting and above all worthwhile. Who's in favour of giving it our best shot?

Language and Politics in a Global Perspective

Mari FitzDuff

Let me start with two unashamed apologies. The first is for speaking in English - and this is not just an apology for this audience, but in fact nowadays an apology I usually make for most of my audiences, who tend to function on the international stage. And my second apology is that I am here not as a linguistic expert, but as someone who is interested, both from a socio-psychological and a politico-psychological perspective, in the whole issue of language in conflict. So forgive me if the nuances of the distinctions and the assertions between languages escape me.

I want to start first by speaking from my own international perspective. I work for a United Nations University (UNU/INCORE) based in Derry/Londonderry. We work in many situations of conflict and everywhere we come up against the problem of language and how it is used in conflict.

Language and conflict

A couple of months ago, I was invited by the Commonwealth and the President of Cameroon to go and talk about diversity and how we approach it. It was organised particularly for the African continent where they're struggling, as we are, and most of the countries in the world are, with issues of pluralism. It happened that I was disembarked at the wrong airport and left 200 kilometres miles away from where I was supposed to be going, in the jungle town of Douala, rather than the capital of Yaounde. I know Africa well enough to know there would be a space between the promises that the President's car would arrive, and the actual arrival. Eventually, even I got frustrated. Being a Westerner, it is quite hard to adjust to African time, so I took out the hundred dollar bills that I usually keep in my bag for such instances and hired a car to drive the 200 kilometres. I was stopped five times on the way to the capital by the Army, who put out wooden barriers stuck with nails to stop our taxi, in order to seek bribes from us. While such incidents are not unusual, what was unusual was that three of the conversations that happened between the driver and the military were asking about me, and about my language allegiance. Although all of these men came from different ethnic tribes, (there are 200 different ethnic tribes in Cameroon), the anger in the conversation was about whether or not I was an *Anglophonie*, i.e. someone who spoke English, and whether or not I was going to meet others who spoke English, while the soldiers, and I suspect the driver, were convinced that French was the language that should be spoken in Cameroon. They are still fighting over who speaks what colonial language in Cameroon.

The second experience concerns the late and greatly-missed Frank Wright, that marvellous scholar from Northern Ireland, and one of the great intellectual provocateurs in the area of conflict. In the late 80's, Frank told me that he was aware that Yugoslavia was about to fall apart. He was a man of great ideals and wanted to go and work in Yugoslavia. So he got himself a set of tapes of Serbo-Croatian in order to learn enough language so that he could go and visit and, if possible, help with dialogue work, which he subsequently did. Unfortunately, soon afterwards, Frank was to discover that he had a brain tumour. (Just after he died, we heard he had bequeathed his whole set of Serbo-Croatian tapes to the Community Relations Council.) By the time of Frank's death, what had happened in the former Yugoslavia was that the Serbs and the Croats had decided that they were not, after all, speaking the same language. When mediators tried to do work there, Serbs and Croats insisted on either using a translator or, if they could not get a translator, they insisted on speaking in English. Within a period of about five years, what had been minor variations in dialect had become an assertion of two languages. Thus is the fate of languages when caught in the politics of conflict.

The other language dilemma with which I am very familiar - because ours is a United Nations University, and we sit with a lot of United Nations bureaucrats - is that, just about 15 minutes before the end of any committee on any topic, the French representative will say 'and now we must make sure we translate the results of our proceedings into French'. And now, just as ritualistically, I will say 'Yes, of course, and for communication purposes we must also translate them into Chinese, Russian, and Arabic and, if we want to translate them into a European language, into Spanish as well so as to service Latin America.' From this you will see that, in the United Nations itself, the whole tension between the function of *communication* and the need for language *assertion* plays itself out at every meeting. Nobody knows how to address it, yet there is a lot of the UN budget being spent on translating most United Nations documents into French, as opposed to languages which most of the population of the world will understand, and where most of the UN related dilemmas are occurring.

Learning about linguistic diversity

Most of us to-day are only learning how to deal with diversity. There are now only about 10% of countries in the world that are basically mono-ethnic, i.e. who have less that 10% of minorities. Most countries are having to deal with this phenomenon, which is caused by refugee movements and economic mobility. A great deal of the work of the *Initiative on Conflict Resolution and Ethnicity* (*INCORE*) is looking at best practice in this area, and we are very aware that most of us are on a learning curve. I would see this conference as part of such learning.

The *Community Relations Council*, of which I was its first Director, also had to embark on such a learning curve, when we were set up in 1990. One of the dilemmas we had was our logo. In the early years, we came up with the idea that our logo should have *Cultural Traditions* on the top and *Duicheas* on the bottom, which is the Scottish Gaelic word for 'Cultural Traditions' We thought we were 'identity-correct', as it were, until we realized there was a significant problem. Most of the people who came here in the 16th and 17th centuries would, in fact, have come from the Lowlands of Scotland, where Scots was spoken, and not from the Highlands where Gaelic is spoken. We had, in our ignorance, considered Scottish Gaelic as providing a possible link between the history of the two communities, but we had not understood that, at that stage, the language question was very much around an assertion of difference, without signalling any aspiration to co-operation. When we withdrew our original logo and consulted on the issue, we came to realise that, in fact, there were 50 ethnic minorities in Northern Ireland and, if they all had their way, we were going to end up with a logo that had about 50 different emblems!

A second incident which I remember well and which challenged our thinking on language was about a district council which, because for the first time ever it had got a nationalist majority, rejoicingly came up with the idea that everybody who answered the phone would say *hello* not just in English, but in Irish. Somebody, however, did some counting and pointed out that there were actually more Chinese speakers in that particular district council than speakers of Irish. So what were the language rights in that situation?

A third issue that used to concern me as Director of the *Community Relations Council* was the fact that we would spend quite a lot of time giving money for translators and machines to facilitate translation into Irish for a great many conferences. However, I attended many conferences where these machines were abandoned after the first five minutes. What happened was that, in the course of the conference, people often became more interested in *communication*, i.e. talking to and with each other, as opposed to involving themselves in *assertion* of their identity. And yet the option for such translation had be to made available in the first place, if people were to feel heard and validated, and thus enabled at attend such dialogue opportunities.

Language as a tool of conflict

What I want to take from those stories is the idea that whether or not a language becomes important politically really does, and this is true internationally, depend on the domestic discourse. In other words, almost all issues can become grist for the mill in a conflict. I've just spent five days in Cambridge with people who were looking at ethnicity and religion as causes of conflict. But of course neither ethnicity itself, nor religion, nor language, is the cause of conflict. And whether any or all of these emerge as issues will depend on the context - usually a context where power is being rearranged, or where people wish it to be rearranged. In such a context, language often becomes a tool with which you sort out other issues. There's nothing intrinsic about it as a dividing factor. So the whole question about competition between languages, or reclaiming languages, which happens everywhere, is usually about competition for power, and for respect and validation. Language, therefore, is often divisive because it is often used as the means whereby to sort out who belongs and who does not, who is respected and who is not, and above all often who has power and who does not. This is why even all the legal safeguards we have will often falter when it comes to the public use of language.

Therefore, and I say this with some hesitancy, because I have just read this morning an excellent paper on the Ulster-Scots language by Manfred Görlach [see this volume], my sense is that, if you are looking at language from a political perspective, there is actually not much point in arguing about the reality of whether what someone speaks is *a language* or *a dialect*, for you are missing the point if you do it. Similarly with the case of Serbs and Croatians: for them to argue that, in five years, they had moved from speaking *dialects* to different *languages* makes little sense - unless you understand their psychological needs in a situation of conflict. This is the same point that we missed over the argument we have had here about the whole question of the Cruithin. Historians here have written a great deal about the issue of whether and when the Cruithin were here - but I never believed that the passions were about realities of history, but about the realities about belonging here, or not belonging here, and the right to feel comfortably at home here.

We can respond through a series of laws, we can look at sliding scale approaches, e.g. in some countries, if it's a 5% minority, you'll get some public rights, whereas, in other countries, the minority will need to be 8% or 10%, and so on. Approaches tend to vary. All of these approaches, i.e. human rights approaches, equality approaches and sliding scale ones, will fail if you miss the underlying human and community dynamics. Equality and human rights debates can be limited. In South Africa, where they have excellent legislation in regard to language, there are eleven official languages, and much debate about the use of these languages. The issues are similar, i.e. when people want to communicate they use English - Afrikaans has now been relegated to one of the eleven minority languages. Unfortunately, what can happen in Parliament is that, when people want to assert, and divide, they will use their own language.

The hegemony of English

I sometimes think the debate about language is the equivalent to the debate that is happening in the churches. As the Christian churches debate amongst themselves about various points of biblical, sectarian and other differences, they often fail to realise that in fact their main enemy is now the secular. One day, they may wake up to find that almost everybody has left and that there are few ears to hear the debate. Similarly with language. Whether one likes it or not - and the French hate it - the language issue as far as global communication is concerned is settled, and it is a language called 'Mutilated English'. In Germany, you now have boards, all of German nationality, who carry out their board meetings in English. And some of you may have been following the debate in California, where we have 50/50 English-speaking/Spanish-speaking communities, with almost every communication in California in double languages, guaranteed by legislation. But recently, there was a huge debate over this with many cases of parents are actually asking that this law be rescinded because they want their children to learn English alone, as they believe their children will thus do better locally and globally What we need to keep in mind as we talk about languages, is that the threat to languages is not actually the differences between us, but the differences, as it were, in the global world where almost all languages are becoming subservient to English.

Language and victimhood

I believe that, while you can have language strategies, which look at laws and regulations, etc., they cannot by themselves address issues of power and inclusion. The term *Jailtacht Irish* (as opposed to *Gaeltacht Irish*) has been used to describe the situation whereby Irish was learned in jail by many Republican prisoners. Many of us are aware of the tension between the *Jailtacht* speakers and other Irish speakers over the political use of the language. If we try and use language to try and solve problems of inclusion and belonging, it can make victims of us all at a very personal level. Recently, a young colleague said to me 'I feel so guilty because I have learnt Spanish and French, and I didn't learn Irish'. This person was suffering from the victimology that many of us now feel in relation to language. I am conscious that many people who have an Ulster-Scots background also feel guilty that they are not taking more seriously the whole concept of Ulster-Scots and teaching it to their children, setting up Ulster Scots schools etc. Such 'identity-correctness' serves well neither us, our communities or the language itself.

Dialogue and gestures: rubbing along

There are however approaches that can help to ease such tensions. I am conscious that gestures are incredibly important - everywhere I go in the world gestures that recognise the 'other' can make a huge, huge difference. I thought we had a significant one here in West Belfast last week, when Steven King, an assistant to David Trimble, started a public talk by a sentence in Irish. Nobody expected him to do any more, nobody expected him to learn Irish, but the gesture was warmly received. Such gestures can make a huge difference. Living in what we call *Derry/Londonderry*, I rejoice when I hear people whose wont is usually to say *Derry*, occasionally to say *Londonderry* where they believe it will affirm their Protestant colleagues and neighbours, because such a gesture can often make a big difference. Everywhere in the world such gestures lower defence levels, and they dissolve the boundaries of antagonism.

We need to learn the value and the low cost of 'rubbing along' rather than 'rubbing out' (as phrased by Mark Adair, see this volume). Basically, we are involved in something that is as developmental as 'rubbing along'. And in language that is probably about all that we will be able to do, and we need to be able to adjust according to the temperature. I am very aware of the negative gut feeling of many Unionists who turn on the radio and hear Irish, and their feeling of betrayal - and indeed the scorn which many people feel towards the use of Ulster Scots. However, the colour and texture of all these languages actually provide for a variety where global communications and the global economy is in danger of wiping out identity. We also need to recognize these explorations and expressions of language are much more important to some than to others. And they are important at different times. Don't let's paint each other into corners over them - such times and such needs will come and they will go. There are probably lots of people who will spend a year learning Irish, or Ulster Scots, sometimes from the Protestant community, sometimes from the Catholic community. Let us give freedom to people to explore. I believe we live in a region where such flexible provision does not cost that much in terms of our overall budgets. And if South Africa, with their limited resources, can afford it, then so can we. Let us look at ways to enjoy our varied languages in terms of gestures or possibilities that often cost fairly little. At this time in our collective history, we need it.

Language as the tip of the iceberg

However, one thing we need to be careful about is that we do not let language ghettoize us, as it does in Sri Lanka and Israel, where different communities, for instance, watch different television channels, and hear different versions of the same news. Education through differing languages can also be very segregating. I am very conscious that, if I had to choose between an integrated school and an Irish school or an Ulster-Scots school, it would be a difficult choice for me personally, given the varying identity and dialogue needs of Northern Ireland. I must admit that I, personally, am very worried by the fact that Catholic schools are beginning to develop Irish schools because this may ghettoise the language still further. Such choices between identity affirmation and mainstreamed cross community education present a real dilemma: if we find we are only listening to people speaking in our language and not hearing the tones and nuances of another, we're actually in danger of separating ourselves, so that we truly cannot hear what the other is concerned about. It is that hearing which is so important in a situation of conflict.

Finally, just to reiterate, we need to remember divisions about language are usually about the tip of the iceberg. If you concentrate solely on addressing such divisions, then you may be avoiding the issues of belonging and power which usually underlie such debates. However, if we address such issues, and give each other space and confidence, then language can be a factor in helping us to move into a society that is not afraid to be both equal and different.

.

Language, Discrimination and The Good Friday Agreement: The Case of Irish

Helen Ó Murchú

Questions to be addressed:

• *Are members of your community (or do they feel) discriminated against on linguistic grounds? Is the discrimination real or perceived?*

• *What expectations do members of your community have of the implementation of the Good Friday Agreement, with its provision of Language Bodies and its strong Bill of Human Rights, with regard to an improvement of the situation and political accommodation?*

Introduction

In answer to the two questions posed, and speaking from a Southern perspective only, within the time constraints, three main points will be made. The answers will be addressed from personal experience of both the 'official' side (past Chair of *Bord na Gaeilge*, the previous Language Board) and the voluntary sector side (chair of several organisations, including *Comhdháil Náisiúnta na Gaeilge*, the steering council of the voluntary sector, and the *European Bureau for Lesser Used Languages*; in my current post, I am working with *Comhar na Múinteoirí Gaeilge*, an organisation for teachers of Irish).

'Real' or 'perceived'?

What may be considered *perceived* is, in fact, very real in the eyes of those who consider themselves the objects of discrimination. In addition, the qualifier *perceived* is often no more than the fallback position of the perpetrators of inequity, be any particular instance real or not.

Terminology may have a role to play in the perpetuation of discriminatory attitudes. That is one reason for the use by the Bureau of *lesser used* as a term. It was first introduced by John Hume in the European Parliament in 1979. The benefits are that it is descriptive of the existing sociolinguistic reality but neither pejorative, as is the term *minority*, nor prescriptive in setting bounds to possible development. It also has the advantage of self-ascription rather than of other-categorisation, as is the case with *minority*, which quite literally means disadvantageous comparison with what is considered bigger and, by inference, better. There are three issues relating to language which must be kept in mind. First, as in the case of *lesser used* and *minority*, uses of language affect perceptions.   Secondly, language is one of the most salient characteristics of difference between communities; it is simultaneously inclusive (for those within the speech community) and exclusive (marking them off from others, and others from them).   Thirdly, language is always a political issue, overt or covert, since it clearly involves questions of differential power.   What is needed are ways of managing that, to the satisfaction of all, through legislation if necessary.

Does discrimination exist for Irish speakers in the Republic?

The plain and simple answer is *YES*!

Some years ago, the Celtic Congress invited me to speak on the position of Irish, North and South.   As framework, the various domains of the Charter of the Council of Europe seemed appropriate as bench marks for such a comparative exercise.   The results were interesting.   Apart from the constitutional position of Irish in the Republic and statutory support structures, such as Government Departments and two semi-state bodies (Language Board and Gaeltacht Authority), the comparative analysis appeared to show that the *difference* between North and South, across all domains, was *one of degree rather than of kind*.   Further, the results showed a marked *concessionary* approach in both jurisdictions.   That is to say, the State conceded to the demands of the Irish language lobby, or voluntary sector, North and South, in different ways and at different times, with regard to education, the arts, public signage, and media.

It is too often conveniently forgotten that Údarás na Gaeltachta (Gaeltacht Authority), Teilifís na Gaeilge now TG4, Gaelscoileanna (Irish-medium schools), Naíonraí (Irish-medium playgroups), and cultural centres all ultimately derive from voluntary sector demand, even though most are now subsumed into the official system.   This may well be democracy at work, but it also shows clearly that discrimination existed, was fought against, and the argument conceded by the State.   The underlying need - that agencies of cultural reproduction must be in the hands of the linguistic community itself - was not really considered as a policy option.

Despite the constitutional position of Irish in the South, Tomás Ó Máille had no lack of material for his work on *The Status of the Irish Language: A Legal Perspective*[1].   There is one case there which concerns the present writer and the organisation for teachers of Irish.   An Irish version of specific forms was needed in order to incorporate the organisation as a limited company.   Two cases had to be taken against the State to ensure their provision: the first to supply them, the second to make the State pay legal costs, which the State considered the responsibility of the organisation which had to take the case to ensure its constitutional rights.   Positively Gilbertian!   The fact that the Government has given consent to the preparation of an Official Languages Equality Bill is proof, if proof were needed, that discrimination exists of a kind that requires legislative action to make the constitutional aspiration practicable.   If and when this Bill becomes law, let it not be forgotten that it was the voluntary organisation

Conradh na Gaeilge (Gaelic League) which began the process by demanding a Bill of Rights.

The constant vigilance of Comhdháil Náisiúnta na Gaeilge is needed to ensure the language proofing of all legislation, e.g. Education Act, Planning and Development Bill.

On the other hand, it must be clearly said that the State in the Republic is neither totally nor solely reactive, even at semi-state level. For example, Iarnród Éireann (Irish Rail), together with NI Railways, have produced a very attractive brochure in Irish on the benefits of taking the Enterprise train to Belfast.

Summary

In respect (in every sense) of human rights, the use of language is clearly an issue. There is need, then, for all measures North and South - being taken, about to be taken, being considered even - to be flexible on the one hand, but to be clearly enforceable on the other. Words in legislation do not remove discriminatory practices. Legislation is no more than the acknowledgement that the problem exists, and hopefully provides some measures to correct or redress the situation. As Irish speakers in the South have found out, the aspiration of the Constitution does not protect or ensure their rights. To date, these have been left to the interpretation of Article 8 of the Constitution made by the judiciary. Legislation may be a much needed beginning, but it will remain a beginning unless forms of implementation and monitoring of results are clearly built in.

Freedom may be negatively defined as the absence of boundaries, barriers, rules. So may real tolerance, for all parties involved. Real understanding of the deeply held beliefs of the other is possible only through a conscious acknowledgement of one's own. To denigrate any group's language is a denigration of language itself.

An Foras Teanga

To examine the issue of the structure of *An Foras Teanga*, one may ask three questions:

- Is *An Foras Teanga* necessary?

- Will *An Foras Teanga* make a difference?

- What will/would make *An Foras Teanga* worthwhile?

To begin, *An Foras Teanga* had an unfortunate birth, quite apart from the stop start situation. Most structures arise out of previously defined plans with clearly defined rather than vaguely couched aims. The hugely political context of the organisation's inception is, on balance, more of a hindrance than a benefit. While commendable efforts were made to have its membership as representative as possible, the public perception still remains that they are political appointees. It did not receive a welcome either North or South, for different reasons. In the South, it was grudgingly accepted in the beginning, solely on the grounds that it might prove of some benefit to the Irish language community in the North. Many elements of that same community saw no need for an additional expensive bureaucratic structure between their existing funding agencies and language promotion activists on the ground. The wording of the legislation only added to existing doubts, particularly in the South. Voluntary organisations, which had hitherto been funded by, and had direct access to, the Government Department responsible for linguistic matters, now found the entire context in which they operated entirely changed. Their fears were compounded by two further factors: not only were they now to be funded by the new structure, but it was patently clear that this was so because officialdom was in fact using this source in order to meet the required budgetary allocation for this imposed structure; the membership, while representing some voluntary organisations, did not compose a forum or entity for the voluntary sector, as proposed in the report *Treo 2000*, commissioned by the Department that was now making these new arrangements. Not alone was this the case, but there now existed a situation whereby some, *but not all*, State-funded voluntary language agencies or ventures were now either to be funded by the new body or had actual representation on it. In addition, some but not all previously Language Board funded organisations had representation. One or other of these elements was present for all voluntary agencies, whether North or South. This potential for possible conflict of interest is a source of unnecessary complication in an already complex situation for a body with an all-island remit. It can only be addressed through a structural solution.

The Language Body is seen as no more than a funding agency. But language promotion does not take place in a vacuum. Choices have to be made. The more acceptable and defendable choices are made as a result of clear language policy elaborated in consultation with those who will be responsible for implementation. This path need not necessarily be all roses either, but it is at least patently transparent and agreed. Policy by cheque is not an answer.

The Body then must communicate its mission clearly so that all can share it and see their role as part of it. This mission should include a practical definition of what bilingualism means in the operational context of the Body. To accomplish its mission, as in the case of any other undertaking, it must establish an appropriate management structure as well as an information base arising out of reliable research that allows for continuous evaluation and flexible change, within the parameters that exist - political, social, socio-cultural. If it is to succeed as it could, *an Foras Teanga* must, above all, establish a formal structured consultative planning context with the voluntary sector. This could well add fruitful effectiveness to too often sterile efficiency.

The Good Friday Agreement saw the need for a Civic Forum. The relationship between State, semi-state bodies, and voluntary language agencies is even more important, particularly if results are sought rather than merely political accommodations between factions. No one has the monopoly on wisdom in language policy! *An Foras Teanga* could, if it is wise enough and sufficiently pioneering, make a breakthrough in this area. The information brochures of the Equality Commission for Northern Ireland, in their different language versions, plead for public involvement in the development of public policy. Will the Language Board do likewise? Preferably, not through a series of public meetings where ideas are noted, but through a permanent pillar within its own structure. The modern state cannot function in any domain without the voluntary sector, the third sector, recognised in France, for example, as a valuable partner. While most voluntary agencies are, to some extent, state agents, they are still independent enough to represent the voice of their particular constituencies to the authorities. Indeed, they must guard against never accepting the State's interpretation of issues without a full understanding of the interests of those they represent. Apart from their function in carrying out some aspects of the State's work - in itself a reason for being involved in policy making - the voluntary sector has other attributes, many of which are detailed in the discussion papers of the Commission of the European Union on building stronger partnerships. The sector functions as:

- public conscience and source of (alternative) ideas
- source of policy
- independent agent
- voice, often of the voiceless
- as focus for those who wish to offer their talents voluntarily to others
- educator and trainer in democratic and civic values

In the new political context emerging, such a pillar would be clear proof of a vibrant *participative* democracy, the elements of which are able to engage in action oriented dialogue towards policy, in a spirit of equal partnership, rather than the unequal, even medieval, relationship of funder and beneficiary.

This would certainly require a responsible attitude towards representativity and pre-partnership among the organisations that constitute the language voluntary sector. In addition, the responsibility for collaboration in helping to create and cost joint policy as well as implementing specific areas of it would be theirs. Given the opportunity, it is not likely that they would fail.

Summary

In the overall linguistic situation pertaining, the words of the eminent sociolinguist, Joshua Fishman, himself no stranger to the Irish case, are apposite. In an address given on his behalf at the Seventh International Conference on Minority Languages in Bilboa in December 1999, he reminded us once again of the intricacies of language.

The utilitarian view is that languages are merely instruments of communication. But any given language is not only symbolic of a given culture but also part and parcel of that culture and its accompanying ethno-cultural identity.

The struggle for cultural democracy, in an age when civil (rather than ethnic) nationalism is being advocated by the centers of power, requires pursuing complex multiculturalism and multilingualism patterns, rather than simple ones.

They bring to mind what has been described in Canada as *The Emerging Consensus* and *Living Together: A Common Purpose.* In the Winter 1992 edition of the magazine *Language and Society*, Victor C. Goldbloom, the Language Commissioner for Canada, who visited *Bord na Gaeilge* and invited its Chief Executive to address the Canadian Parliament, had much to say in his editorial that is of direct relevance to us here and now, North and South, with much of which we can sincerely empathise. It is worth quoting in full.

In Canada *(read whichever place you wish)*, with almost two and a half centuries *(read your own estimate)* of linguistic coexistence in English and French - and more than four and a half centuries of far from perfect relations with the Aboriginal peoples - we face special challenges and special opportunities. For a considerable time now we have been expending effort and emotion on talking about texts and structures. Now it is essential - especially in the aftermath of the referendum *(read Agreement)* - to focus on human beings and human relations. Canadian society is characterised by its diversity, and out of that diversity we must distil some measure of cohesion and co-operation, some sense of common purpose. Whatever constitutional decisions *(read Bill of Human Rights)* may eventually be arrived at, we live next to one another, and we shall have to talk to one another. Knowledge of our own and others' aims and motives, of our histories, both shared and disparate, is essential. We need clear, honest dialogue, expressed in clear, honest language. Canadians are known for settling their differences in a civilized way, in a fashion that is the envy of others, but we must not expect instant satisfaction or instant accomplishment, nor lose patience or our sense of commitment. We must not perceive our linguistic duality as a zero-sum game, one in which no one can win unless someone else loses. A country or a confederation or a common market cannot be built on bitterness. Despair is not a policy; resentment is not a basis for human relations. Relations must be based on fairness and equity: equity in employment, equity in advancement, equity in participation in the life of our society. They must be based on understanding, especially of our historical roots and the present-day emotions which underlie our various concerns and objectives. They must be based on mutual courtesy and mutual consideration. The vast majority of Canadians are decent and caring people. We must make a continual effort to point out, to sustain and reinforce, what is positive in people's attitudes and personalities. It is better to light a single candle than to curse the darkness.

Let us articulate clearly our common purpose, together. In doing so, we need to understand and to know more about the linguistic milieu in which we exist. Much of the saner debate, for example, on Ulster Scots has centred on the argument regarding *language* and *dialect*. Erik Allardt points out that the term *dialect* 'has a socio-political content since it contains an element of subordination.' [2] There are some objective linguistic criteria for distinguishing dialects and languages. These tend to reify language. It is useful then to consider also the more subjective attitudes, perceptions, beliefs and intentions of the actual community of speakers, whether this community be in territorial or personal terms. This, of course, presupposes the existence of some specified or specifiable community. The agencies devoted to Ulster Scots might then consider a sociolinguistic survey to determine the extent of this community and its current perceptions of linguistic and cultural needs, in conjunction with the proposed purely linguistic-based work on corpus aspects. The *Dualchas* project based at the Gaidhlig-medium third level college on Skye, Sabhal Mor Ostaig, is currently collecting and digitising existing materials in Gaidhlig and Scots. Ulster Scots might benefit culturally and technically from joining this venture.

There are languages other than English, Irish and Ulster Scots spoken in both the Republic and Northern Ireland. It is useful then to distinguish between autochthonous (from the Greek *chthonos* meaning soil, land) or historical languages and the languages of migrants, particularly those recently arrived. A question hangs over when, after how many generations, does a migrant language become indigenous.

The relative constitutional status of Irish and English in the Republic allows both to be *official* but only one to be *national*. In fact, it is by virtue of its being considered the national language that Irish has the status of first official language. This *national* status is very important to many people, both North and South.

The present Irish language community is composed of both Gaeltacht speakers, speakers from Irish-speaking households and increasingly, of second language speakers generated through the education system, particularly through Irish-medium schools. The majority of the latter come from English-speaking homes and, in common with other reported cases of school generated competence in L2 for majority language speakers, a specific register or variety has arisen which is perfectly adequate for communication purposes with others in the same situation. This has given rise to the phrase *Gaeilge líofa lofa*, or awful fluent Irish. If allowed to calcify, this could have future consequences for Irish, particularly in light of a reducing Gaeltacht core. Two further aspects of this changing situation have been noted.

1   Language loyalty is not some abstract dreamed up by language revivalists. It is to the local variety, be that in a Gaeltacht region or in a city such as

Dublin or Belfast. Despite the efforts of scholars, the notion of a spoken standard has not really taken hold in the unusual situation of three main regional varieties of (more or less) equal social prestige.

2   Children of Irish-speaking homes in urban areas who attend Irish-medium schools appear to control at least three registers: the school register used for communication with peers of mixed language background (in order not to appear 'culchy' was one explanation given); the register used in the home; the register used in communication with Gaeltacht speakers in a Gaeltacht setting.

In the changing political and structural context in which we now find ourselves as speakers of our languages, the opportunity exists for communication with each other on levels that were not there before. Unless those opportunities are wisely used, the future gulf could prove unbridgeable. We expect much, both of ourselves and others, and yet are afraid to hope.

Notes

1   Tomás Ó Máille. *The Status of the Irish Language: A Legal Perspective* (Dublin: Bord na Gaeilge, 1990)

2   Erik Allardt. 1984. In *Journal of Multilingual and Multicultural Development*. 5:196. [*Proceedings of the Second Conference on Minority Languages*]

Language, Discrimination and the Good Friday Agreement: The Case of Ulster-Scots

Ian Parsley

I would love to open with a sentence in Irish, but unfortunately I haven't got beyond is *maith liom ceathratha ceol*. I would, however, like to say a few words in Scots. Firstly, I should point out that what I am about to say is the product of a consultation exercise with *Ullans-L*, the e-mailing list which I run, and from other discussions.

Sae, the baith quaistens [see p. 79] *A hae tae gie a repone tae, wud be the ae quaistens as the 'Airis' delegation wud hae tae gie a repone tae an aa, bean gif thai be discrimination, rail or thocht o, agin Ulster-Scots taakars (bean taakers o the Braid in Ulster); an whit the futur o Ulster-Scots wud be efter the 'Guid Fridey Greement'. It wud be gey fur giean a repone, fur thai ir nae Ulster-Scots taakan communitie. Thai ir Ulster-Scots acteevists, an Ulster-Scots taakars, bot thaim twa wud be gey differ. Sae, wha wud be thair representars? That is gey sweir an aa. Bot it is clear at the Ulster-Scots souch wudna be thocht o as uissfu fur wark an thrift, ye wudna heir it in furthsetin, on television or the radio. An it bes gey sweir finndan fowk fur tae uise it.*

A wus doon in Dublin last yeir, A haed tae gie a recordin fur the Agnes Burns Heritage Centre in Drogheda, an we haed tae finnd a wumman. It wus gey sweir finndan a bodie at wud uise the Braid tongue in the apen. A haed askit a haill wheen fowk roon bae Belamenagh, roon bae Caulrain, we cud finnd niver a ane at wud dae it. Sae A taen ma auld mam, an we taen the siller atween us!

Thon's a gey muckle problem, an we hae tae owrekim it. The guidein o the Civil Sairvice forby is a problem, A'm no fur sayan ocht agin that. Thai wud be a wee bit want o ken. Aiblans thai wud be lane ten executives fur the Airis side, bot thai wud aa taak the Airis. Wae Ulster-Scots it bes gey sweir finndan fowk as taaks the Scots fur tae wirk in the onkim o Scots. Thai wud be the problem an aa o the siller gien oot fur Scots - nae mair nor millye pun. It's gey sweir daean ocht fur the onkim o the tongue, a place in the seistem o lear wae nae siller. It wud be gey sweir an aa whaniver public bodies juist lauch at you. A wus at a public bodie no sae lang syn, whar the wumman juist leuch at the notion o Ulster-Scots in the seistem o lear. The Government o Airlann forby haesna yit gien thair signatur tae the Charter o the Cooncil o Europe. Sae, Ulster-Scots (or Scots) wud be nou hae leid richts in Norlin Airlann, bot no in Dinnygal. A wee bit orra. A wee bit beter nor whaniver hit wus a leid in Scotlann bot no in Airlann, bot it's no parfit yit.

Unner the Belfast Greement, whit richts haes the 'Ulster-Scots speaking community'. That is gey sweir tae gie a repone tae an aa, fur thai ir a differ atween Ulster-Scots acteevists/taakers in the Coontie Doon an the Coontie Antrim. In the Coontie Antrim, the Braid Scots is yit tae finnd. Thai ir monie taakars in the Coontie Antrim, an thai ir nae rail danger in this generation at the leid bes fur daean oot. Bot in the Coontie Doon, hit is sweir tae finnd. Thai ir a Braid Scots souch, bot nae rail Braid Scots gremmar, fur ensample. Sae the onkim o the Scots cultur fowkgates in the Coontie Doon wud be linguistic, in the Coontie Antrim hit wud be anent the cultur. Thar we hae muckle sangs an makars o indyts, bot owre in the Coontie Doon thai wud be mair concarnt wae finndan auld wurds, names o places, an daean a wee bit wae auld saws an the lik.

The Bill o Richts is no yit tae finnd neither, fur we irna sae sicar whit bes fur kythean in it anent the Scots speak in Ulster.

The negative pynts (an it wud be gey rare fur an Ulster Scot stertan wae negatives!), wud be want a ken an nae dutie gien tae fowk as haes the skills necessar fur the onkim o the Scots 'linguistic side' baith ben an but academia. Forby, thai ir fears o bias, fur ensample whaniver screiveins maks mentions o the Airis in Norlin Airlann an no the Scots.

Thai ir positives forby, bot. The Charter o the Cooncil o Europe wud be the importanmaist thing at haes cum aff wae the Scots tongue in Scotlann an in Ulster, A am thinkan, aiblans in the last fower hunner yeir. Thai ir forby, wae the 'Cross-border Language Bodies' the mechanisms fur larnan fae whit kims aff wae the Airis in Norlin Airlann an in Dinnygal, an we can larn fae that that. Thai ir an owreaa ploy an aa fur the Ulster-Scots Leid Societie, at gies an owreaa wey o whit wey we ir fur forderan the speak, the leeteratur an the cultur. A am thinkan at we ken at the leid canna gae on athoot the cultur an at the cultur canna gae on athoot the leid. In the ploy sud kythe a wee bit anent the leid in the seistem o lear in Norlin Airlann, an aiblans in the Republic forby, an anent the bringin in o mair as haes the Scots as thair hamelie tongue intae the owreaa muivement, sae it's no juist 'governed' fae Belfast. It's gey important at the haill muivement wudna be 'Belfast-centric'.

I will finish off in English with a brief overview of the situation. I would agree, first of all, that I'm not sure there's such a big difference between real and perceived discrimination. If discrimination is perceived, then it is real. Whether you can say that the Ulster-Scots speaking community as a whole faces discrimination is arguable, because there's nobody to represent the whole community or to explain what discrimination there is. However, there is discrimination against Scots speakers in Ulster, and against the Ulster-Scots accent in general. Under the Belfast Agreement, we do have an opportunity to move forward. We will either take that opportunity 100%, or we will fail. But I think the most important ten years are the most important ten years. If there is no agreement on how to further develop Scots speech and literature in Ulster, then we cannot really expect to get very far. But, if we can come up with an agreement and involve those with relevant skills, and by that I mean particularly those currently studying issues related to Ulster-Scots at postgraduate or undergraduate level, we might just have a chance. The most important thing of all is to involve those who actually speak Ulster-Scots, and to get away from ridiculous language/dialect debates almost entirely based in Belfast.

Language, Discrimination and the Good Friday Agreement: The Case of Sign

Bob McCullough

The Facts

There are approximately 4,000 deaf people in Northern Ireland whose first language is sign. The greater majority of these deaf people are profoundly deaf and the average reading age when they leave school is nine.

This means that my eleven year-old hearing grand-daughter has better English, a richer vocabulary and a greater amount of general knowledge than the average deaf adult.

Deaf people are very much aware of the poverty of their education and, until recently, have just accepted it as one of the penalties of being deaf. They have no say in the education process and are now demanding greater involvement in decision making.

The word *deaf* has many different meanings but, for the present purpose, I will dwell specifically on those who were born deaf and have no knowledge of sound.

Nine out of ten deaf babies are born to hearing parents who have no knowledge at all of deafness and are unable to communicate. This means that, for the first three years of the child's life, it is missing out on the sub-conscious learning that builds up the vocabulary in normal hearing children and stimulates their minds to learn words and gather facts and information.

A profoundly deaf child needs the stimulation of communication just as much as a hearing child. We in the deaf community are angry that the advice given to parents always comes from hearing professionals who, we believe, are often biased against sign language and, in advocating the oral approach, are depriving deaf children of the stimulus they need in the first three formative years of their lives.

Deaf children born to deaf families have this communication and stimulation from the time they are born because the parents naturally know the best way to communicate - by body language, sign and gesture. Children in this position have the chance to develop their potential and, if bright enough, achieve the same educational success as their hearing peers.

With the Bill of Human Rights promising empowerment as well as equality of education, deaf people are asking to be included in the decision-making process. We feel that in spite of all the problems, deaf people of the right calibre can succeed if good teaching and a supportive home background have the communicative help required.

Deaf adults who have missed out on education can also benefit from this enlightened policy. No more second-class citizens but, through BSL and skilled interpreters, full partakers in the joys and responsibilities of life.

Discussion

Parents of deaf children are given conflicting advice by social workers and educational officials on the best way to educate deaf children. For many years, this was a simple choice between the oral/aural system, in which no signing is used, and the Total Communication approach, which uses sign, finger spelling and gestures along with lip-reading, in an attempt to give the children full and clear understanding of language. This has now been superseded by what is termed 'bilingualism'.

Deaf people had no say in the method used, and generations of deaf children, unable to benefit from the enforced use of hearing aids and oralism, were condemned to low grade education through no fault of their own. Education failed them, not because of their inferior intelligence, but because the communication method used frustrated rapid assimilation of information and denied them the stimulation and encouragement they needed. A certain percentage of deaf children were able to take advantage of the oral/aural approach because they had enough residual hearing to benefit from the hearing aids provided. This emphasises my point that education must be adapted to the child as the word *deaf* has so many different meanings and hearing aids are of little or no use when the audiogram registers 90 decibels or over, the mark usually accepted as the threshold of profound deafness.

The advocates of oralism and auralism maintain that English as a language needs to be built up in the brain through repeated exercises, and that sign language brings in a contradictory set of images, which prevent deaf people acquiring the language of their country and condemns them to separation from mainstream language acquisition. Deaf children who do well academically are sent to the Mary Hare School in Berkshire, where the oral/aural policy is enforced, and these bright children are given the opportunity to progress to GCSE and A levels and obtain entrance to university. We have no grammar school like this in Northern Ireland, and many parents do not like to see their children leave home at the age of eleven for education in an overseas college, even though they recognise the high academic standards of Mary Hare and similar institutions.

The situation in deaf schools is changing rapidly. Many old schools are closing and the deaf pupils assimilated into mainstream education with, in some instances, sign language assistance where needed. New and powerful hearing aids have enabled many children to have almost normal reception of the spoken word, and these pupils are able to compete on equal terms with their hearing peers. Added to this is the rapidly expanding number of cochlear implants (in Northern Ireland alone over 50 children have received this operation), and many parents are now coming to the conclusion that special education is unnecessary and their children will be able to cope with normal schooling.

In parallel with this changing scenario, we are seeing a new interest in after-school learning, and many deaf adults have come back to further and higher education in their twenties and thirties and have shown that, with proper teaching and interpreter support, they are perfectly capable of achieving their goals. But this has to be qualified with the understanding that the loss of the normal build up of information through the sub-conscious mind that hearing children enjoy has left large gaps in their vocabulary and grasp of concepts which are very difficult to surmount, and means that the search for new knowledge and qualifications may take longer than expected.

My own position is that deaf people will never be equal with hearing until they are as well educated as they are. I also feel that BSL has been given a mystical status that tends to absorb too much of some deaf people's time and prevents them buckling down to education so that they may acquire the qualifications needed for progress in the real world.

Does Sign Language Need Official Status?[1]

Deaf people from all over the British Isles have been campaigning for official Government recognition of British Sign Language (BSL) and large crowds marched through London in July 2000 claiming that BSL was one of our largest minority languages and should be acknowledged as such.

Chief spokesman for the campaign is Doug Alker, London based leader of the Federation of Deaf People and a former chief executive of the Royal National Institute for Deaf People, who believes that recognition of BSL would improve everything from education to employment and open the doors for deaf empowerment in social and government bodies. Doug is an inspirational speaker with much support from certain sections of the deaf community. He has recently published a new book setting out his ideas and explaining why he disagreed with the RNID and had to part from them. I met Doug in Belfast some years ago and had a long chat with him. An old boy of Mary Hare, he has been active in deaf TV programmes and is an undoubted master of sign language and amateur dramatics, which he used to good effect to make us all laugh in the Deaf Comedians, a group he helped to establish, which has toured deaf centres both here and on the mainland.

But in my writings and on TV, I have always maintained that BSL is a language of communication and cannot be recognised as an official language because it has no written form.

I believe with all my heart that deaf people will never be able to claim equality with hearing until we are as well educated as they are, and to achieve this we need a better command of the English language.

I agree absolutely that deaf people have been badly treated by the education system. One of the prime reasons for this is a failure to achieve better communication both at home and at school during the children's most impressionable years. Many deaf children have been wrongly placed in hearing impaired units where they were simply unable to cope and missed years of basic education, which left them unable to catch up later.

Doug would maintain that we need more deaf teachers, and he could be right; but I am sure he would agree that we could have unsatisfactory deaf teachers as well as unsatisfactory hearing ones, that quality is all-important, and that the ability to use sign language will not by itself produce well-educated children.

I have helped teach deaf adults and know how much they long for a better command of English. The world is now more literate and communication for us has improved with minicoms, e-mails, mobile phones with text, and subtitles on TV and videos. When interviewed for magazines deaf people are often asked if they prefer subtitles or sign language, and the answer is invariably subtitles.

Added to this is the continuing decline of deaf schools and a rise of deaf children in mainstream settings where English is the dominant medium. Parents of deaf children are now much more aware of the options before them and are seeking the best education available.

Advocates of BSL say it is a language in itself with its own structure, its own idioms and its own linguistic history. I do not argue with this, but I do insist that it is a language without books and incapable in itself of enabling deaf people to achieve the potential which their intelligence and natural ability equips them.

Do we really want to belong to a small minority arguing forever about our rights and ignorant of the rapidly changing world with its plethora of information through books and newspapers and the wonders of the internet?

I welcome BSL interpreters in educational settings and for communication with doctors and other officials. But I cannot see us having any meaningful part in higher office until English is recognised as our first and most essential language.

Conclusion

To quote from my *Deaf Talkabout* column in the *Belfast Telegraph* (6.9.00):

> The important thing is that hearing folk have made all decisions on the education of deaf people for the past 100 years and the results have often been disastrous. We now have a growing number of deaf adults with university or business training, and it is time they were given the chance to determine future policy.

An Alternative View by Jeff McWhinney[2]

I agree with Bob McCullough (*Belfast Telegraph*, 27.9.00) that deaf people will not be able to claim equality with hearing people until the standard of education received is improved. However, the official recognition of British Sign Language is a fundamental part of this.

The British Deaf Association has been campaigning for many years for the Government to officially recognise BSL. We believe that bilingual education, where a deaf child is taught in BSL and English, is essential if all deaf children are to reach their full potential.

It will surprise many people to learn that deaf children do not receive a standardised education and many receive teaching only in English, resulting in school-leaver literacy levels much below that of the UK average.

Purely oral/aural education has severely damaged the education of a significant number of deaf people. The BDA finds this unacceptable, and while we applaud Mr McCullough's assertion that a better standard of education is needed in the deaf community, we know that this is not achievable without BSL being used alongside English in education.

Mr McCullough also refers to the inappropriateness of legalising a language without a written form. However, there are a number of languages without a written form, which are recognised legally in many parts of the world.

Endowing BSL with official legal status would ensure that funds are allocated for language learning It would also lead to a greater number of sign language interpreters in the UK, enhancing the quality of life for the deaf population.

The BDA will continue to campaign until this objective is achieved.

Notes

[1] Reproduced from my *Deaf Talkabout* column in the *Belfast Telegraph*, 27.9.00.

[2] Jeff McWhinney, Chief Executive of the British Deaf Association, Letter to the *Belfast Telegraph*, 14.11.00, setting out the position of those who want official Governmental recognition of British Sign Language.

Language, Discrimination and the Good Friday Agreement: The Case of Cantonese

Anna Man-Wah Watson

Cantonese speakers in Northern Ireland

Cantonese is the second most spoken language in Northern Ireland. This fact may surprise many people, but it's true. Cantonese is a dialect of Chinese, which is spoken daily by about 8,000 Chinese people here in Northern Ireland, many of whom cannot speak English or speak very little English. The Chinese Community is the biggest ethnic minority group here and, yes, they do feel excluded, and they do feel discriminated on linguistic grounds. I remember an elderly man once stood up in a public seminar and he said 'I became deaf and dumb when I came to live in Northern Ireland'. This can be said for many of the Chinese people here in Northern Ireland.

In Northern Ireland, we are simply not very good at catering for citizens whose first language is not English. Why? Unlike the rest of the UK in many cities, public information here is very rarely translated into community languages. We talk about food scares and meningitis epidemics, but nothing ever gets translated into Cantonese or Hindi or any other language for its citizens. There are literally hundreds of leaflets in Northern Ireland about the entire range of health care services available in the National Health Service, but very few of them have ever been translated into any other language. Information taken for granted for speakers of English is very seldom given to ethnic minority people who need the information desperately. When they use the services of GPs, hospitals or social workers, many Chinese people need interpreters.

In the Chinese Welfare Association, we employ three interpreters for the whole of Northern Ireland, i.e. 8000 people. It's not enough. People are still using children, friends and relatives to translate for them in situations when they need the privacy and confidentiality which is provided by professional interpreters. People refrain from going to seek medical care because they are unable to find friends or relatives to go with them.

Cantonese and education

The majority of Chinese people start Primary 1 with very little English because their parents only speak Chinese, and many of them find themselves being left at the back of the classroom to sink or swim, as it were. In our schools, there are no policies and very few resources to help children whose first language is not English. Recently, 40% of teachers claimed they have come across children whose first languages is not English and confirmed that there is such a lack of resources, and that they have had very little training themselves to cope with these children. Many of the children really do suffer. We are increasingly seeing the second generation of Chinese children coming out of school with few qualifications and few job prospects and who are therefore going back into the catering trade. Bilingualism in English and Chinese is not recognised in our schools. Teachers take it for granted that children whose parents are Chinese must speak both languages, Chinese and English. It is not recognised that it is wonderful to be able to speak the two languages, but this is not the reality. Some parents are told to stop speaking Chinese to their kids and to speak English to them. But there are two difficulties with this advice: firstly, the parents don't speak English. Secondly, the parents want their children to speak Chinese too. It is a real and not an ideological issue because the parents want the children to be able to communicate with them and, if they don't teach the children Chinese, they won't be able to communicate with each other. We are seeing examples of that now, with some Chinese children acquiring English and forgetting a lot of Chinese, and creating a big gap in communicating with their parents. You can imagine the difficulties of parents and children not being able to communicate in a common language.

There is a Chinese-language school in Belfast with 200 children every Sunday learning to read and write Chinese. It is very much based on a community effort - the State has not done very much to support the group. There is a few hundred pounds every year from the Belfast Education and Library Board, but it is very much down to the community, to the parents to organise it.

Is Cantonese an after-thought in the Good Friday Agreement?

The Good Friday Agreement has emphasised the importance of respect and tolerance in linguistic diversity. It includes Irish, Ulster-Scots and also, for the first time in Northern Ireland, there is official acknowledgement of the languages of the various ethnic communities. We are very much waiting to see the impact, the outcome of it like, for instance, supporting Chinese-language schools. Yes, we are hopeful about the Good Friday Agreement, we welcome the various aspects of it, we welcome the broadening of the equality agenda. For the first time, Northern Ireland is not simply talked about as a community of two traditions, it's beginning the broadening out of the equality agenda to include race and other constituencies. We are hopeful that it's going to raise awareness, that it's going to give us some clout to lobby. We welcome, too, the establishment of the Equality Commission and the Human Rights Commission. They have worked very well with the Chinese Community so far in terms of consultation and finding the needs of the Chinese Community. We are hopeful too about the Section 75 under the Northern Ireland Act, placing a statutory duty on public bodies to carry out their functions with due regard to equality of opportunity and, in particular, giving public access to information and services. We can certainly use that for the benefit of the Chinese Community.

All in all, we are hopeful about the elements of the Good Friday Agreement, although we are concerned and worried about the implementation of it. Are the ethnic minority needs going to be a second thought again? We feel we are grateful when we are included in anyone's agenda. There is a recent exhibition organised by the Linenhall Library called the *Languages of Ulster*, and we got included as a second thought. *Languages of Ulster* is immediately thought of as Irish and Ulster-Scots, and ethnic minority languages are very much thought of as an add-on. So we are hopeful that the Good Friday Agreement is not going to be a tokenistic gesture to include ethnic minority people here. To be a truly inclusive society, we need to be thinking of Northern Ireland not as a place of two traditions, but as a place of a multi-cultural society.

Language, Discrimination and The Good Friday Agreement: The Case of Ethnic Minority Languages

Nadette Foley

It is timely that the question of ethnic minority languages is being considered at this seminar in terms of the protection offered by the Good Friday Agreement. The exact wording of that document specifies its relevance to 'both communities' in Northern Ireland. I hope that these discussions can move the issues of language discrimination out to a broader set of linguistic communities present within this society.

As someone working with people from minority ethnic backgrounds, I am not speaking as an expert on linguistics or even on language rights. Today, listening to the earlier speakers, I have picked up some new language, the language of talking about language rights. In the current work that I do at the *Multi-Cultural Resource Centre-Northern Ireland* (MRCRC-NI) and in my previous work with asylum seekers and refugees in the Republic of Ireland, the language issue comes up, but it is not seen or thought of as a separate one. The language element is embedded in the whole question of trying to adapt this society both North and South, to put in place the infrastructure necessary for a multi-cultural society. In the programme for today's discussions, minority ethnic languages, are down as 'non-indigenous languages'. This can be interpreted as a very negative and exclusive term, and we have heard from the *European Bureau of Lesser Used Languages* of their gentler, softer use of the phrase 'lesser used languages', and I will take that away with me from today's discussions. Generally, we talk about 'minority languages', which seems to suggest a hierarchy of languages.

Following on from what my colleague Anna Watson from the Chinese Welfare Association has said [see this volume], I would not want the new dispensation, the new equality context and the proposed Bill of Rights to suggest that there should be such hierarchies. There are over thirty - and perhaps up to fifty - different languages spoken in Northern Ireland today, and these have to be considered equally. The people who speak them have to be invited to the table as equals to discuss language rights. The issues for speakers of Irish and Ulster Scots may hinge mainly around the expression of cultural identity. For the small percentage of the population who speak the other lesser used languages, it is a matter both of having the rights to engage with the statutory system in your mother tongue, and of wishing to strengthen and maintain your cultural identity.

The role of the Multi-Cultural Resource Centre is very much a bridging one. We work with all individuals who perceive themselves to be from an minority ethnic background. We encourage people to name themselves, because very often people are put in boxes and identified as 'the Chinese community'. There may be an assumption that there are homogenous groups who are Chinese, Indian, Pakistani or Muslim. In my work, I find that there are individuals who come from very mixed ethnic and linguistic backgrounds; when you look at a particular community, such as the Bangladeshis, you see that the language issue is very complex.

As an example, the MCRC-NI wished to produce an audio tape aimed at signposting the basic health and social services available in Northern Ireland as a resource for the Bangladeshi community. We always seek expert advice from agencies in England, Scotland and Wales who have had previous experience with the same language group. We contacted an agency in Preston to ask which language they would use and they said that Bengali was definitely the majority language. A contact in the Bangladeshi community here told MCRC that there seemed to be a large proportion of Sylheti speakers. The difference may reflect an urban, rural and class divide. We then contacted a group in Tower Hamlets who seemed to have a similar demography to the population here. They explained that, if we used Bengali, we could really alienate the Sylheti speaking people who come from rural Bangladesh, who would feel that we were catering for the needs of the more privileged Bengali speakers and ignoring the majority grouping. This has been a learning experience, which shows us that we must be extremely sensitive in making such decisions.

It is often necessary to consider producing multi-lingual materials in audio or video formats as people may not be literate in their mother tongue. In addition, people from the second or third generations may have learnt the language orally from their parents, such as Cantonese, Hindi, Arabic or Farsi, but they have not necessarily had the access to parent-run mother tongue schemes. They will not have the ability to read their own languages in the original script. Some such materials on general health issues produced in other parts of the UK are useful here. The MCRC-NI holds copies of audio and video tapes which can be borrowed by individuals or professionals for use with clients, such as a video on childbirth or an audio tape on how to stop smoking in several languages. Under Section 75 of the Northern Ireland Act 1998, it will be for local statutory bodies to fund the production of materials specific to Northern Ireland. The DHSS&PS and the EHSSB and NHSSB have already begun to contribute to this work through the Minority Ethnic Community Health and Social Wellbeing project of the MCRC-NI.

On a wider scale, it is important to recognise that there is a huge diversity among the communities who speak these lesser used languages. What makes this a very different issue to that of Irish or Ulster Scots is the completely fluid linguistic communities involved. There are new people constantly coming to settle in Northern Ireland, and the demography is changing rapidly. A 1995 MCRC-NI booklet on language and cultural information about the main minority ethnic communities here did not include the African community because it was not considered numerically significant at that time. It now numbers over 1,600. The groups that make up both the Muslim and the African communities are very diverse linguistically and yet they share some common cultural characteristics. The only guidance is that you have to be very open and sensitive, and there needs to be a dialogue with speakers of these languages.

Earlier speakers have talked about the language rights debate at the United Nations and the power issues that have developed. Within the EU, I would see a similar position, with the officially designated EU languages all being traditional European languages. However, the EU has very large populations of Turkish, Kurdish, Arabic, Cantonese, Hindi and Punjabi speaking communities who are living, breathing, working and bringing up generations of new communities, and yet there is no official recognition of language rights for them. That is my question for the Bureau of Lesser Used Languages. When are we going to accept these newer languages as indigenous? The Hindi/Punjabi speaking community in Northern Ireland is going into a fourth generation. What do we mean by 'indigenous'? These languages are around us within the EU, and they are actively part of the linguistic landscape here. That presents us with a challenge, particularly in the light of the NI Peace Agreement.

We now have the 1997 Race Relations Order, the Equality Duty of Section 75 of the Northern Ireland Act 1998, and the proposed Bill of Rights. There is a difficulty in presenting the needs of the communities who speak these lesser used languages in Northern Ireland as these people are already alienated and socially excluded in this society. Minority Ethnic People and Travellers have been identified as specific categories within the Promoting Social Inclusion initiative. They come from very different cultures and may not even have expectations of having their basic rights and needs fulfilled. As my colleague Anna Watson has explained, there are life and death issues regarding access to information in your own language, and that is often the most immediate difficulty that is presented by the people with whom we work.

There is research in parts of the UK which suggests very strongly that mother tongue education is wonderful in terms of confidence building, so that children will access the English curriculum and also the entire primary curriculum at a much higher level, and will succeed better academically if they have mother tongue provision. Reading those results has changed my own attitude. I used to think that mother tongue was a nice luxury. When I worked in Dublin with many refugee communities, even the life and death interpretation and translation issues were not catered for. At that time, there was no English as a Second Language support at primary level for children of asylum seekers. When I first heard about the mother tongue school for the Cantonese and Mandarin speaking children in Belfast, I thought it was interesting. It was not an issue for any of the refugee communities in Dublin except those invited by the Government, for whom State funding was available for mother tongue classes on Saturdays. With regard to parents, information on the UK research on mother tongue provision and its effect on educational attainment is not disseminated in Northern Ireland in the relevant languages so that parents can actually own the expectation that the Government will subsidise and support them to run mother tongue schools. The parents need to be facilitated to engage in an equal dialogue with the statutory bodies and the Government. The challenge for the MCRC-NI and all other organisations in this field is how to empower people to become involved in the equality debate at an equal level and not to ensure that this issue is not a Cinderella one within the larger language rights debate in Northern Ireland.

Some children are now studying Cantonese or Arabic at GSCE or A levels. Given the importance of international languages for the future growth of IT based employment in Northern Ireland, the communities which speak these major world languages should be seen as having rich potential to produce part of this vital future workforce. Particular attention should be given to the diversification of language teaching at second level. Vocational training and access to employment and education courses will also need to be adapted to allow for speakers of English as a Second Language. MCRC-NI, in co-operation with Belfast Women's Training Services, has begun to provide the Women Moving On course in personal and professional development, accredited with the Open College Network for a diverse group of women from different linguistic backgrounds. This requires linguistic support and particular sensitivity to participant's language needs.

The Chinese community is very self-reliant and have become organised by training each other to represent their issues well at conferences and seminars. The Indian community has also recently started Hindi mother tongue classes. The Asian families group in Craigavon holds Koranic Arabic classes as does the Islamic Centre in Belfast. Some of the smaller communities such as the Latin Americans and the Bangladeshis and others do not yet have community organisations. The Albanian speaking Kosovars have come as asylum seekers and have had to struggle to obtain permanent immigration status. These groups are here and should have high expectations that the system will adapt to their linguistic diversity. However, they do not have that expectation, yet.

There are also acute language needs within the justice system. Dealing with family abuse or other sensitive issues, it is often necessary to seek an interpreter or translator from outside Northern Ireland because it may not be appropriate to use someone from within a very tiny linguistic community for reasons of confidentiality. This is also true in asylum advocacy work. Five years ago, while I was working in Dublin, it was difficult to find a speaker of Albanian with good English in Belfast,

The Home Office used to contact me to request the services of a colleague, whose father was ethnic Albanian, to travel to Northern Ireland to interpret for asylum interviews. Recently, the MCRC-NI has had to suggest an interpreter from the Republic of Ireland in an instance of family abuse within a small minority ethnic community here. The difficulty in dealing with the statutory sector is often one of critical mass and, because the Chinese community can say they have 8,000 people speaking Cantonese, they have got further with the authorities than other language groups. The modest progress made in employing some community interpreters is, however, still not enough. The other communities are not even at the starting gate and this is why Section 75 presents us with unique challenges and opportunities. It should not matter about numbers but about reducing inequalities. If there is one woman who has to use their young daughter to interpret in an interview with a gynaecologist, that is one woman too many. The difficulty will be how to adjust existing resources to these needs and that may be where the equality duty will fall down.

What MCRC-NI is trying to do is to create a space for dialogue on multi-lingualism, particularly in the health and social services sector. We do this by bringing together the statutory policy makers with people from the different linguistic communities. On a positive note, we now have the Section 75 Equality Duty leaflet published in nine languages, including Irish and Ulster Scots and Urdu, Cantonese and other lesser used languages. The Eastern Health and Social Services Board has also issued its recent Racial Equality Policy in several languages with a multi-lingual summary. It is a question of us all continuing to challenge the statutory bodies and Government to give recognition to multi-lingualism. It is also important to make the small gestures, to have a welcome poster in 30 languages in a reception area, to have different faces on publicity materials, and particularly for staff to be trained to react sensitively and listen to what someone's language needs are. The language rights debate which has been given a new energy by the equality and human rights provisions of the Good Friday Agreement gives the minority ethnic communities a valuable opportunity to articulate their specific needs. The challenge now is for each of us to accept some responsibility for the adjustment to a future multi-lingual society.

Language, Discrimination and The Good Friday Agreement: The Case of Gays

P A MagLochlainn

As a former grammar school language teacher, and now as President of the Northern Ireland Gay Rights Association, I have long had an interest in the still-invisible gay teenager, all too many of whom never survive the trials of our education system to become adults. As a life-long trade unionist, and an active involvement in amateur dramatics, I fully realise the power of language to persuade or to hurt.

I hope to give you some idea how language is used to discriminate against our community. There are many people who deny the existence of a gay community, to which my usual response is that we definitely do exist as a "community of disadvantage", easily identified by our enemies, such as gay-bashers, who on occasions regard any member of our community as fair game for their "policing operations".

It is true that our community lacks many of the common denominators of other communities – we have no geographical base, unless you count the gay quarters of certain cities. Even Belfast is now developing its own gay village in the Cathedral Quarter, where we have all the major gay venues. Gay householders also tend to congregate in certain areas of the city, such as the rich glitterati-land of Stranmillis, or the bohemian student-lands of Malone and the Ormeau Road beyond the bridge.

Because our minority is not as visible as (say) the coloured and ethnic minority, or the Travelling People, that does not make its existence any the less real. I am constantly bemused by the number of visitors who "do" Northern Ireland in two or three days with a camera, but who never talk to the natives, and thereby miss the single most unusual – and yet characteristic – feature of society here. I refer of course to our unique "stained-glass apartheid", whereby perfectly normal citizens of Belfast can go most of their lives without ever once having a real, honest encounter with a member of "the other sort." A lot of people here live their lives like the bishops on a chess-board, whose dioceses appear at first glance inextricably interwoven, yet who never meet, for one move forward on the black squares, and the other is permanently confined to the white.

Since our special Northern Ireland version of apartheid is not coloured black and white, nor as obvious as the racial differences of the United States, most visitors come and go entirely unaware of this absolutely crucial chasm between the two halves of our community. They never notice that this is the only society in the world where most towns have not one, but two, newspapers in the same language.

I use the expression "gay community" to include not only gay women and men, but also most minority sexual groupings such as bi-sexuals, transsexuals and transgendered people, as well as the transvestite community (who are overwhelmingly straight in sexual taste, but whom majority society "lumps in" with all other sexual minorities). As I said earlier, all of our minorities have in common the fact that we are disadvantaged (to greater or lesser degrees) by the majority society.

The "policing operations", to which I already referred, do not necessarily take the form of physical gay-bashing. Verbal gay-bashing is a lot more prevalent, and often even more deadly in its effect. Classic Catholic theology distinguishes three ways of telling a lie – by word, deed or omission. Most of the sins committed against our community are those of omission.

Thus we gays are routinely written out of history. Every approved text of our society, from fairy-tales to school texts, always feature compulsory heterosexuality. When teaching children about James Baldwin, for example, why is it that of all his works, it is ALWAYS *Go Tell It On The Mountain* which features on the school curriculum? Simple – because that is his only novel in which homosexuality is not crucial.

Our society sins by omission also when parents or grown-ups simply ignore something a child has said or asked, and pass on. It would be worth exploring the theory which I have sometimes come across, which holds that one finds a higher percentage of 'out' gay people among deaf teenagers and those in their twenties than among their hearing contemporaries. The theory has it that these young deaf gay people miss the "policing" effect of the silence used by many parents, teachers and others in authority in order to lie about gayness and gay people.

For too many youngsters desperately seeking the truth, this conspiracy of silence does indeed prove fatal. This child finds no help or support from its parents, its school ignores it or tells lies about it, its doctor shows no signs of understanding, its church condemns it to hell. The gay child is probably the most isolated child in our whole society, at precisely the period in its life when most teenagers passionately want to belong to their peer-group. Death is often preferable to such a wretched existence. That is why gay activists shout "Silence equals Death".

One of the most insidious forms of this deadly silence is the pretence that young people are NEVER gay, but that gay citizens suddenly appear over-night like a fairy ring of mushrooms on a lawn. Any attempt to assert that schools do in fact have gay pupils and should in all justice cater to them is met with accusations of homosexual propaganda against innocent children. The legal system, and judges in particular, cling to the hoary and totally discredited myth that teenagers can "be led into making a choice that they will regret for the rest of their lives". Even a cardinal can talk about "teaching" children about "the theory, or the practice, of homosexuality." I wish I had the fortitude of the Christian martyr who murmured "Sancta simplicitas" on a similar occasion - but all too often I think angrily of millstones around necks for such as harm innocent gay little ones.

Our society is, in fact, teaching children about homosexuality from the cradle. If the baby boy is more attached to his doll than to his gun, Daddy begins to worry. Primary school children regularly call one another *faggot, fairy, fruit, homo, lezzie, pansy, poof, sissy,* etc. They may not know exactly what these terms mean – but they are certainly fully aware that these terms refer to something no-one ever wants to admit being. Schools which punish pupils for shouting *nigger* or *kike* (or even occasionally *gyppo*), will merely smile when the gym master lashes his boys to greater efforts by calling them *ladies* or *sissies*.

By the time sex education begins in school, the damage is already done – and is often permanent. Study after study has demonstrated that gay girls and boys are many times more likely to attempt suicide than their peers. We have no way of questioning those youngsters who succeed in killing themselves, but it is logical to deduce that a large number of these deaths have occurred because of our society's use of language to discriminate against its gay citizens.

Should a Bill of Rights for Northern Ireland Protect Language Rights?

Tom Hadden

[At the Symposium, Tom Hadden gave an oral presentation based on a pamphlet prepared by the Northern Ireland Human Rights Commission as part of its consultation on possible guarantees for language rights in a new Northern Ireland Bill of Rights. With a few omissions, the full text of the pamphlet is as follows. Eds.]

Under the Good Friday Agreement and the Northern Ireland Act 1998, the Northern Ireland Human Rights Commission[1] has been given the task of advising the Secretary of State on a Bill of Rights for Northern Ireland. The Agreement also says that the Bill should reflect the particular circumstances of Northern Ireland and the principles of mutual respect for the identity and ethos of both communities and parity of esteem. The exact wording of the relevant paragraph from the Belfast (Good Friday) Agreement is reproduced in italics:

The new Northern Ireland Human Rights Commission will be invited to consult and to advise on the scope for defining, in Westminster legislation, rights supplementary to those in the European Convention on Human Rights, to reflect the particular circumstances of Northern Ireland, drawing as appropriate on international instruments and experience. These additional rights to reflect the principles of mutual respect for the identity and ethos of both communities and parity of esteem, and—taken together with the ECHR—to constitute a Bill of Rights for Northern Ireland.

Among the issues for consideration by the Commission will be:

- *the formulation of a general obligation on government and public bodies fully to respect, on the basis of equality of treatment, the identity and ethos of both communities in Northern Ireland;*

- *a clear formulation of the rights not to be discriminated against and to equality of opportunity in both the public and private sectors.*

One of the questions which the Human Rights Commission has to ask itself is whether and, if so, how language rights should be protected in a new Bill of Rights. This paper tries to deal with some of the issues which arise for consideration in this context.

The Good Friday Agreement makes express provision for the recognition and promotion of both Irish and Ulster-Scots and a cross-border body with executive powers has already been established to carry out that commitment. In addition, the UK Government is committed to ratifying the European Charter for Regional or Minority Languages in respect of Irish. The major question is whether any further protection regarding the use of minority languages needs to be included in a Bill of Rights for Northern Ireland.

European Developments

Throughout its consultation period the Commission will have to keep up to date with developments in human rights law in Europe. There is currently a proposal for a new European Union Charter of Fundamental Rights, which may address a broad range of civil, political, economic, social and cultural rights. However, whether and how such a Charter will be enforceable locally is at present unclear. The European Union is also in the process of producing new Directives aimed at protecting people more effectively against discrimination, particularly racial discrimination and discrimination within the sphere of employment. The Council of Europe, likewise, has drafted a new Protocol to the European Convention which will provide additional protection against discrimination. If a coherent human rights framework is to be provided for Northern Ireland, a Bill of Rights for Northern Ireland must clearly take into account not only the existing European Convention but also the potential developments mentioned here.

Issues for Consideration

- *What languages other than English are regularly spoken by communities in Northern Ireland ? What barriers do non-English speakers face in our society?*

- *What does the European Convention on Human Rights say about language rights?*

- *What will be the practical impact of the ratification of the European Charter on Regional or Minority Languages?*

- *What additional protection will be provided by the cross-border body set up under the Good Friday Agreement?*

- *What additional rights could be provided in a Northern Ireland Bill of Rights?*

- *Should we have the same rights for all languages?*

- *What obligations would be imposed on others if specific rights for minority language speakers are granted?*

(a) What languages other than English are regularly spoken by communities in Northern Ireland? What barriers do non-English speakers face in our society?

Most of the public debate on language issues has been focused on the status of the Irish language and more recently on the status of Ulster-Scots. Government researchers have reported that some 140,000 people claim to be able to speak or understand Irish. There are no equivalent figures for Ulster-Scots and some people claim that it is more of a dialect than a distinctive language, though it has been recognised as a minority language by the European Bureau of Lesser Used Languages. But no-one argues that those who speak Irish or Ulster-Scots, or even Gammon (the language of some Travellers), cannot speak or understand English. The position of those whose mother tongue is Chinese or Urdu or another 'foreign' language is often different. Many of them cannot speak or understand English well or at all.

The position of those who rely upon sign language must also be borne in mind. Many people argue that sign language is itself a different language, using concepts and syntax different from those employed in English. Sign language users often prefer even written documents to be in such innovative forms rather than in standard English, in order that the concepts being explained can be better understood. In Northern Ireland, both British and Irish sign language are used.

So there are three very different groups of people whose rights must be considered:

- English speakers who want also to have their right to use Irish or Ulster-Scots recognised or guaranteed;
- Those whose mother tongue is not English and who may not be able to speak or understand it;
- Those who rely upon sign language to communicate.

It is clear that the same set of language rights would not be appropriate for all these groups.

(b) What does the European Convention on Human Rights say about language Rights?

The European Convention on Human Rights does not specifically provide for language rights. However, some of its provisions are significant for indigenous and minority language users.

For example, Article 6, which deals with the right to a fair trial, provides that everyone charged with a criminal offence has a right to be informed promptly in a language which he or she understands of the charges against him or her. Such a person also has a right to the free assistance of an interpreter if he or she cannot understand or speak the language used in court. But this would not include a right for someone who understands English to use Irish or Ulster-Scots in court.

Other Articles in the Convention might be particularly useful to people who face restrictions on their use of a minority language or are discriminated against because of their use of the language. Article 10, which guarantees the right to freedom of expression, could be relied upon in a challenge to any legislation which tried to prevent anyone from using their own language for their own private purposes. But this would not give any general right for those concerned to insist on using their own language for public purposes or to insist that public officials should understand it or respond to them in it. Article 14 of the European Convention - which prohibits discrimination in the enjoyment of the rights and freedoms in the Convention on any ground such as sex, race, colour, language, religion, political or other opinion, national or social origin, association with a national minority, property, birth or other status - has been interpreted by the European Court of Human Rights in a similar way. It does not require the state to take any positive action.

The provisions of Article 2 of Protocol 1 in respect of education are also unlikely to be of much help to those who want their children to be educated in Irish or another minority language. It provides that 'in the exercise of any functions which it assumes in relation to education and to teaching, the State shall respect the right of parents to ensure such education and teaching in conformity with their own religious and philosophical convictions'. But the European Court of Human Rights has held that this does not cover a right to education in a particular language. And in any case the UK government has entered a reservation to this Article, stating that it will apply it only to the extent to which it does not require unreasonable expenditure.

In summary the European Convention provides only for:

- a right to use a particular language with friends and socially, without government interference;
- a right not to be discriminated against on the basis of being a minority language user;
- a right to interpretation and translation in a court, where that is necessary to understanding the proceedings.

(c) What will be the practical impact of the ratification of the European Charter for Regional or Minority Languages (1992)?

The Charter provides for extensive positive duties to be imposed on states with regard to what the Charter defines as regional or minority language, that is languages that are:

- traditionally used within a given territory of a state by nationals of that state who form a group numerically smaller than the rest of the state's population;
- different from the official language(s) of that state.

But it does not include either dialects of the official language(s) of the state or the languages of migrants. Nor does it seem to cover the needs of those who rely upon sign language.

The Charter is very broad in the type of measures it contemplates. But it allows states a wide choice of which of these measures to implement for a particular language. There are two levels at which states can commit themselves. At the lowest level states are required under Part II of the Charter to accept some basic principles in respect of all languages which meet the definition of a regional or minority language:

- to recognise the value of the language and promote its study;
- to take resolute action to promote its use;
- to foster cross-border links with other users of the language;
- to foster mutual understanding between users of minority languages and the national language;
- to avoid any discrimination against the language.

The higher level of recognition under Part III of the Charter requires states to commit themselves to at least 35 specific measures of recognition and promotion out of a possible list of about 100 options in respect of education (26 options), judicial proceedings (15 options), administration (21 options), media (15 options), culture (10 options), economic issues (9 options) and trans-frontier links (2 options).

The British Government has recognised Irish and Ulster-Scots under Part II of the Charter and has undertaken to ratify Part III of the Charter in respect of Irish in Northern Ireland. But it has not yet published the 35 measures which it proposes to adopt. It appears, however, that the choice will be limited to those forms of recognition and promotion which are already being provided.

It should be noted that recognition under the Charter is limited to Irish and Ulster-Scots and that the Travellers' language and other minority languages used by immigrant groups, such as Chinese and Urdu, might not qualify even under Part II. In any event, ratification of the Charter does not give the users of a minority language any direct right to enforce the commitments which have been accepted. Rights granted under a Northern Ireland Bill of Rights, on the other hand, would be enforceable in local courts.

(d) What additional protection will be provided by the cross-border body set up under the Good Friday Agreement?

The Good Friday Agreement contains a number of specific provisions in respect of the recognition and promotion of Irish and Ulster-Scots in Northern Ireland:

> *All participants recognise the importance of respect, understanding and tolerance in relation to linguistic diversity including, in Northern Ireland, the Irish language, Ulster-Scots and the languages of the*

various ethnic communities, an of which are part of the cultural wealth of the island of Ireland.

... the British Government will in particular in relation to the Irish language, where appropriate and where people so desire it:

- *take resolute action to promote the language;*
- *facilitate and encourage the use of the language in speech and writing in public and private life where there is appropriate demand;*
- *seek to remove, where possible, restrictions which would discourage or work against the maintenance or development of the language;*
- *make provision for liaising with the Irish language community, representing their views to public authorities and investigating complaints;*
- *place a statutory duty on the Department of Education to encourage and facilitate Irish medium education in line with current provision for integrated education;*
- *explore urgently with the relevant British authorities, and in co-operation with the Irish broadcasting authorities, the scope for achieving more widespread availability of Teilifís na Gaeilge in Northern Ireland;*
- *seek more effective ways to encourage and provide financial support for Irish language film and television production in Northern Ireland; encourage the parties to secure agreement that this commitment will be sustained by a new Assembly in a way which takes account of the desires and sensitivities of the community.*

As with the ratification of the European Charter, however, these commitments are not directly enforceable in the courts.

(e) What additional rights could be provided in a Northern Ireland Bill of Rights?

There are many issues for indigenous and minority language users which are not covered by the European Convention on Human Rights or which are not directly enforceable under the European Charter for Regional or Minority Languages or the cross-border arrangements established by under the Good Friday Agreement. Some of these are issues about the rights of individuals to use their own language in dealings with public bodies. Others are about how far the government should go in providing positive support for a language.

There are different degrees of positive recognition and support which could be given to languages and language users in a Bill of Rights. Rights for individuals, for example, could include:

- a right to use the language and to be answered in it in some or all dealings with public bodies;
- a right to use the language in court proceedings even if those concerned are able to understand English;
- a right to use the language and to have simultaneous translation facilities in the proceedings of public bodies such as the Assembly or local district councils
- a right for parents or children to be educated in schools in which a particular language is the main language of instruction.

Rights for more general support could include:

- providing access to education for learning the language (for example, through schools or evening classes);
- funding bodies to promote the language;
- providing public facilities and services, such as health care, in the language in question;
- providing radio and television services in the language at state expense.

(f) Should we have the same rights for all languages?

It is obvious that it would be impractical to guarantee the same rights for the users of every language which is or could be used in Northern Ireland. No-one could sensibly argue that, for example, a speaker of Swahili or Estonian should have the same rights as a speaker of Irish, and there are no international human rights conventions which would support any such claim. The more important issue is what the criteria should be for the inclusion of rights for particular languages.

As has been explained, the European Charter for Regional or Minority Languages draws a distinction between languages used by indigenous communities and those used by immigrant communities. This would suggest that Irish, Ulster-Scots and perhaps also the language of Travellers should be given some positive recognition over and above what is provided in the European Convention on Human Rights. But many more people in long-established communities in Northern Ireland use Chinese and Urdu than Ulster-Scots or the language of Travellers and as a result they may be less able to access various services about which information is provided only in English. In creating rights for language users, should some account therefore be taken of the number of people who regularly use a particular language?

A further issue is how the general principle of parity of esteem between the two main sections of the community in Northern Ireland should be implemented in respect of language. Should the Irish and English languages be given the same status as official languages in Northern Ireland as in the rest of Ireland under the Irish Constitution? Or should Irish and Ulster-Scots be given the same subordinate status to English as the national language? The British

Government is already making a distinction between the degree of recognition and support it gives to Irish and Ulster-Scots both in respect of the ratification- of the European Charter and in the cross-border arrangements established under the Good Friday Agreement.

(g) What obligations would be imposed on others if specific rights for minority language speakers are granted?

A further related issue is the extent of the obligations which would be imposed on others by the grant of enforceable rights in respect of languages other than English. To what extent would public bodies have to facilitate the use of another language? Would several officials in each public body or office be required to be able to understand it and respond in it? Would a central service be required to field queries and responses in, say, Irish? Would all public officials be required to learn Irish or other languages? Should different areas have different levels of requirement, such as in designated Gaeltacht areas in the Irish Republic? And should any obligations at all be imposed on individuals in the private sector, for example in shops and financial institutions, to provide facilities in languages other than English?

These are important practical issues which must be given serious consideration, not least since they may involve substantial expenditure.

Appendix: Examples from other Bills of Rights

The European Convention on Human Rights (1950), Article 14:
The enjoyment of the rights and freedoms set forth in this Convention shall be secured without discrimination on any ground such as sex, race, colour, language, religion, political or other opinion, national or social origin, association with a national minority, property, birth or other status.

International Covenant on Civil and Political Rights (1966J, Article 27:
In those states in which ethnic, religious or linguistic minorities exist, persons belonging to such minorities shall not be denied the right, in community with the other members of their group, to enjoy their own culture, to profess and practise their own religion, or to use their own language.

The Constitution of the Republic of Ireland (1937), Article 8:
(1) The Irish language as the national language is the first official language. (2) The English language is recognised as a second official language. (3) Provision may, however, be made by law for the exclusive use of either of the said languages for any one or more official purposes, either throughout the State or in any part thereof.

The Canadian Charter of Rights and Freedoms (1982):
Section 16: Official languages of Canada
English and French are the official languages of Canada and have equality of status and equal rights and privileges as to their use in all institutions of the Parliament and Government of Canada. [A series of specific sections provide for proceedings and communications to be in both languages].

Section 23: Language of instruction
(1) Citizens of Canada (a) whose first language learned and still understood is that of the English or French linguistic minority of the province in which they reside, or (b) who have received their primary school instruction in Canada in English or French and reside in a province where the language in which they received that instruction is the language of the English or French linguistic minority population or the province, have the right to have their children receive primary and secondary school instruction in that language in that province.

(2) Citizens of Canada of whom any child has received or is receiving primary or secondary school instruction in English or French in Canada, have the right to have all their children receive primary and secondary school instruction in the same language.

(3) The right of citizens of Canada under subsections (1) and (2) to have their children receive primary and secondary school instruction in the language of the English or French linguistic minority population of a province (a) applies wherever in the province the number of children of citizens who have such a right is sufficient to warrant the provision to them out of public funds of minority language instruction; and (b) includes, where the number of those children so warrants, the right to have them receive that instruction in minority language educational facilitates provided out of public funds.

The Constitution of South Africa (1996), section 6:
(1)   The official languages of the Republic are Sepedi, Sesotho, Seytswana, siSwathi, Tchivenda, Xitsonga, Afrikaans, English, is Ndebele, isXhosa, and isZulu.

(2)   Recognising the historically diminished use and status of the indigenous languages of our people, the State must take practical and positive measures to elevate the status and advance the use of these languages.

(3)   (a) The national government and provincial governments may use any particular official languages for the purposes of government, taking into account usage, practicality, expense, regional circumstances and the balance of the needs and preferences of the population as a whole or in the province concerned, but the national government and each provincial government must use at least two official languages.

(b) Municipalities must take into account the language usages and preferences of their residents ...

Note

[1] Northern Ireland Human Rights Commission, Temple Court, 39 North Street, Belfast, BT1 1NA; Tel: +44 (0)28 9024 3987; Fax: +44 (0)28 9024 7844; Email: nihrc@belfast.org.uk; Website: www.nihrc.org

Institutional Infrastructure Post-Good Friday Agreement: The New Institutions and Devolved Government

Seán Farren

It is my pleasure, personally and as a Minister in the Executive, to attend and contribute to today's session of this conference. Personally, I am very pleased because my master's degree is in linguistics. As a result and also working in teacher education at the University of Ulster, I have taken a keen interest in aspects of the debate about language issues in Northern Ireland over the past three decades. As a member of the new Executive, which has as a fundamental aim consolidating the peace process by, amongst other things, promoting mutual understanding between our different cultural traditions, I am pleased to participate in a conference debating issues very relevant to the achievement of that aim.

Indeed, this conference must be one of the most wide ranging in scope and in importance on the whole question of language and society ever held in Northern Ireland.

In my presentation, I want to concentrate on the principles and parameters within which the new political institutions are required to operate, and then to mention some of the practical measures already being undertaken with respect to those principles and parameters.

I have to stress, however, that, while the Executive took office last December, the lengthy period of suspension from February to the end of May meant that progress in developing policies and programmes within the context of the principles and parameters which I will outline has been seriously delayed. It is only now that the process of formulating a programme for government, within which common policies will be elaborated and programmes developed, is proceeding. It is a process that will not be completed until the close of the year.

I must also stress that, since I am not the Minister directly responsible for cultural and linguistic matters, and since policy and programmes directly attributable to the new Executive are only beginning to be formulated, I am somewhat constrained in what I have to say about what will be done.

The 'manifesto', if I can refer to it in that sense, under which the Executive has taken office, is the Good Friday Agreement. That agreement sets out the principles to which I have just referred. Primarily those principles impose commitments to developing *"partnership, equality and mutual respect as the basis to relationships within Northern Ireland, between North and South and between these islands"*.

Applied to the issues of concern to this conference, these commitments require a recognition of the *"... the importance of respect, understanding and tolerance in relation to linguistic diversity, including in Northern Ireland, the Irish language, Ulster-Scots and the languages of the various linguistic minorities, all of which are part the cultural wealth of the island of Ireland"*.

This obligation to recognise, respect, understand and tolerate our linguistic diversity, is a major challenge. Indeed in light of the 'health warning' issued by Manfred Görlach (see this volume), the challenge is one surrounded by many sensitivities and possible dangers.

It is a challenge to those who would try to deny that such diversity exists, to those who would grudgingly admit that such diversity is limited to only two languages, English and the second, Irish, being just about worthy of acknowledgement. It is a challenge to those who would celebrate Irish as the only other language worthy of recognition alongside English. It is a challenge to those who would talk disparagingly about Ulster-Scots, whether as a language or a variety of another language. It is a challenge to the Ulster-Scots community itself who might not all be as welcoming of the kind of attention some are giving to their culture at the present time. It is a challenge to those who would not have acknowledged any need to take account of the languages of communities hitherto not indigenous to our shores.

In summary, the challenge is to acknowledge that Northern Irish society is a more linguistically diverse society than many would previously have been prepared to accept. Secondly, the challenge is to move from that acknowledgement and acceptance to making public space for, and allowing resources to be devoted to, practical measures which will enable public recognition and expression to be given to our linguistic diversity and to the cultural diversity of which that linguistic diversity is a part. All that at the same time as we are engaged in a process of creating and developing closer links between the people who espouse the traditions that make up this diversity.

The task facing the Executive, therefore, in light both of the Good Friday Agreement and of the soon to be ratified Council of Europe's Charter for Regional or Minority Languages, is to develop policies, programmes and support mechanisms which will promote that public recognition and expression.

In addressing the issues related to linguistic and cultural diversity identified in the Agreement, the Executive is, of course, not starting with a blank sheet, nor is it addressing a uniform situation with respect to the language situation.

With respect to the latter, we have a situation of considerable linguistic imbalance. English is our dominant language and the first language of an extremely high proportion of those born here. Where it is not the first language, it is probably soon acquired - out of necessity, if for no other reason.

Irish is the second language, with at least 140,000 persons indicating some knowledge of it, passive or active. The use of Irish as a public medium is most regular within the educational domain in the growing number of Irish medium schools, at second and primary levels as well as nursery/pre-school level. Business, commercial and administrative uses of Irish are developing but are not at all extensive. A limited range of Irish medium programmes are being produced for local radio and television. Irish is seldom heard on the streets except in a limited number of areas and by a small number of people.

Nevertheless, there is a vibrant Irish language community in Northern Ireland with links to the wider Irish language community in the rest of Ireland and now extending those links especially to the Scots-Gaelic communities and to other communities within the Celtic family.

Ulster-Scots is much less researched as to the number of speakers and its use, while public awareness of it is clouded in ignorance and, for some people, in considerable prejudice as well.

Also within our society there are those of the non-indigenous communities using, as their first language, languages of China and of the Indian sub-continent, among others. Furthermore, if, as the South has begun to experience in recent years, we were to experience the arrival of other non-indigenous people, we could see that list rapidly expand.

As far as the situation prior to the Good Friday Agreement is concerned, developments were already under way on several fronts, primarily addressing the needs of the Irish language community and, if funding is a measure of what was happening, doing so mostly with respect to Irish medium schooling.

But, as already indicated, the Good Friday Agreement has given a new impetus, a new dynamic and new responsibilities to the whole issue of language diversity. The new institutions established under the Agreement reflect some of that change.

Perhaps the most important initiative taken since the Good Friday Agreement was the establishment of the Department of Culture, Arts and Leisure as the lead department for language policy as set down in the Agreement. The Linguistic Diversity Branch of that Department is the unit of the administration most closely involved in the elaboration of general language policy.

In terms of policy and programmes, the Department of Education has a special remit for Irish medium education at pre-school, primary and secondary levels.

My own Department, the Department for Higher and Further Education, Training and Employment, has a more indirect supportive role given that, unlike the Department of Education, it does not have direct responsibility for curricula either at university or further education levels, or indeed within training programmes.

Research is supported by my Department through the general funding arrangements for universities, not directly to specific projects.

Within the Office of the First and Deputy First Ministers lie responsibilities for human rights, equality and community relations, each of which touches on aspects of culture and language as set out in the Agreement.

With respect to the European Charter, Steering and Working Groups have been set up to decide how it should be implemented for Northern Ireland and, specifically, which provisions of Part III of the Charter apply to Irish. This part of the Charter outlines *"Measures to promote the use of regional or minority languages in public life ..."*. The Groups are widely representative of the departments of the devolved government and also include the Northern Ireland Office and the Courts Service. The work is being taken forward by the Linguistic Diversity Branch of the Department for Culture, Arts and Leisure, assisted by a consultant to the Council of Europe.

Other initiatives prompted by the Agreement are those relating to extending reception of the South's TG4 channel to Northern Ireland, about which technical discussions are ongoing.

A two-year Irish language TV and film production pilot scheme will start by April 2001. Officials of my own Department are in discussion about the kind of training support which the various technicians involved in Irish language film production may require. Irish medium education, especially at pre-school, primary and secondary levels, is one of the issues within the whole context of linguistic policy arising from the Agreement to receive attention.

Currently the Department of Education funds eight Irish medium schools (seven primary and one secondary) with approximately 1,500 pupils. There are also two grant-aided Irish medium units located within English medium schools, with a further two to be grant-aided from next month. Approximately 300 pre-school places are currently being assisted with funding from the Department of Education.

Comhairle na Gaelscolaíochta (the Council for Irish Medium Schools) is being established to advise on policy and oversee its implementation in this area. Among the issues which it will address are the viability criteria for new Irish-medium schools. This is an issue with considerable potential for controversy, and one which requires a balance to be struck between factors such as the capacity to provide for the whole curriculum, the cost of separate facilities, the cost of staff, and, most important of all, the capacity to ensure the overall educational and social development of the pupils attending Irish medium schools. As one who received almost all of my own primary and second level education through the medium of Irish, I need no convincing of its positive value.

Initiatives with respect to Ulster-Scots include financial support for the Ulster-Scots Heritage Council to employ an Education Officer together with agreement in principle to provide resources to support strategic development work. Academic research has been commissioned by the Research Branch of the Office of the First Minister and Deputy First Ministers to establish a sound knowledge on the geographical distribution of Ulster-Scots and on public attitudes and perceptions.

With respect to other ethnic groups, a Working Party on the Position of Minority Ethnic People will identify unmet needs and other factors which can cause minority ethnic people to be at risk of social exclusion and provide recommendations for cross-departmental policy and strategy. Language is not specifically mentioned, though it is likely to be raised as an issue if social exclusion is to be effectively addressed. However, I accept that merely viewing such languages as these groups use in the context of social exclusion, while necessary, may well be seen as a very narrow perspective. Such a perspective says nothing about fostering, celebrating or promoting such languages, and these are legitimate expectations in the light of the Good Friday Agreement. Other initiatives are, therefore, likely to be necessary to achieve a more comprehensive approach to minority ethnic cultures and their languages.

Perhaps the most headline setting initiative under the Agreement has been the establishment of the North/South Language Implementation Body with its two linked agencies, *Foras na Gaeilge* (the Irish Language Agency) and *Tha Boord o Ulstèr-Scotch* (the Ulster-Scots Agency). This Body will be in the forefront of many initiatives' complementing those taken by our own new Northern Irish administration and extending its range of activity across the whole of the island. Building on decades of experience of Irish language development and promotion, a great deal is expected of it

To date one Ministerial meeting of the Body has taken place. At board and official level a great deal of preparatory work is underway. The Body has a budget of just under £8,000,000 this year made up of contributions from both administrations.

In terms of wider relationships between the people of these islands, the British-Irish Council offers possibilities for supporting initiatives within the whole area of cultural and linguistic relationships.

In conclusion, I want to stress the importance, for the whole Good Friday Agreement, of the obligations to promote understanding and respect for our cultural diversity and, within it, for the linguistic diversity we possess in this society. That diversity, in addition to being understood and respected, should be celebrated as a great and positive part of our heritage. For too long, we have not all wanted to see our heritage in its rich complexity. In its mosaic of Irish, Scots, English, Celtic, Norman and Anglo-Saxon traditions, with traces of Nordic, French Huguenot and perhaps many others, combining now with wider European and North American and even Asian influences, all daily transforming us.

Let us use our talents within this new dispensation to acknowledge and celebrate the best of the past so that in all its positive respects it can be part of the reforming and transforming process that we have to go through if we are to live in a society, as the Good Friday Agreement says, imbued with a spirit of reconciliation, tolerance and mutual trust.

Language and Politics: A Perspective from Scotland

Alasdair J Allan

Tha mi glè thoillichte a bhith ann an Eirinn an diubh aig Oilthigh a Bhanrigh, agus tha mi'n dòchas gum bidh co-labhairt math aig a h-uile duine an seachdainn seo.

A'm richt gled ti be here the day at Queen's universitie, an A hope ye aw hae a guid collogue this incummin week.

I have not yet given anything away about my politics or my religion, at least not by my use of either Gaelic or Scots.

The use of Irish or of Ulster Scots in Northern Ireland is of course more politically charged. While I claim no specialist knowledge of either of the minority languages in Northern Ireland, I hope I can mention some of the more obvious points of contrast between Scotland and Northern Ireland, particularly with regard to national identity. I'll also mention how the Scottish Parliament has made an impact on the language situation in my country.

Everything I say comes with a health warning. I am a political animal, a Scottish Nationalist, and I now work for the SNP's Shadow Minister for Culture, Broadcasting and Gaelic.

Anyway, in Scotland, the identity contrast is not really between people who are Scottish and people who are British. It is more between people who are primarily or only Scottish, and people who have a dual Scottish-British identity. The other important point, of course is that the political debate in Scotland is not a conflict between two fixed communities.

Take the example of my family, who all come from fairly similar religious and social backgrounds.

My grandparents are simultaneously Scottish and British - British to the extent that one grandmother has been boycotting German goods in the shops since 1918. My father and I are certainly not British, and my mother is still making up her mind.

National identity in Scotland is not primarily conditioned by religion or social group, but by age.

In 1979 McCrone and Paterson's survey was still able to find 38% of people in Scotland who classed themselves as "more British than Scottish". By 1999, that had declined to 17%. Other polling evidence suggests that these 17% are almost totally in the over 45 age bracket. There has been a corresponding increase in the number of Scots who say they have no British identity at all.

I am of course speaking about what we might call the "Scottish question". The different stances which some people in Scotland take on Irish politics is another matter altogether, and represents the kind of identity clash more familiar to people in northern Ireland.

In Lanarkshire, North Ayrshire, parts of Glasgow and West Lothian, there certainly do exist tensions between Protestant and Catholic identities. But that has nothing much to do with how these people vote on the Scottish question. For instance, the percentage of Roman Catholics voting SNP at the last election was practically identical to the national average.

That has not stopped people attempting to link the two national questions. In the Monklands by-election in 1994, some Labour canvassers were said to have warned Roman Catholic voters that, if the SNP ever got a Scottish Parliament, it would be "like the old Stormont". The same Labour canvassers were also said to be warning Protestant voters that "home rule is Rome rule".

All that shows is that the Scottish and Irish questions in Scotland don't tie up in any very obvious way. And I cannot stress strongly enough that in the vast bulk of Scotland, religion, football and politics are *not* an indivisible trinity.

For instance, my grandfather is a Church of Scotland elder, a Presbyterian. He is also a lifelong Celtic fan. Growing up in the Borders, I was unaware – as he probably still is – that those two identities contain any potential contradiction.

Indeed, I remember when I was about 14, one of my classmates went to an Old Firm game in Glasgow and encountered the whole sectarian thing for the first time. When he got back home, he decided he would give it a try. So, in class, he made a derisory remark directed at the Queen. When asked for an explanation by his teacher, he hesitated and said, "weil, she's a Catholic – is she no?". None of us in the class – Protestants or Catholics - were quite sure, and my friend's career in sectarianism fizzled out there and then.

As I said to begin with, language does give away much about religious or political affiliations.

The Gaidhealtachd is represented by parliamentarians of all political parties, including, since the advent of proportional representation, Conservatives.

As to religion, a native Gael could quite easily come from the most conservatively Presbyterian end of the Church of Scotland or from breakaways from that church, like the Free Church, or the ultra-conservative Free Presbyterian Church. (Not to be confused with Dr Paisley's Church of a similar name!)

A Gael could just as easily, however, be a Roman Catholic from Barra, South Uist, Benbecula, or other pockets of the Highlands, which remained almost untouched by the reformation.

Although the vast majority of Catholics in Scotland have family who came to Scotland from Ireland in the last 150 years, the Gaelic speaking Catholics are a notable exception.

The politics of a native Scots speaker requires, of course, some definition. If we restrict ourselves to the more traditional rural dialects, which have a greater autonomy from standard English, then the rural Lowlands have traditionally voted Liberal or Tory. The advent of the SNP since the 1960s has, however, complicated that, and these are now the areas where the SNP wins its first past the post seats.

Paradoxically again, however, that is not where the SNP gets most of its votes – those now come from traditional Labour heartlands. If our definition of Scots extends to cover the urban dialects, then it also covers many Labour voters.

The fact that I am a native Scots speaker does not mark me out as anything in particular religiously, either. I suppose the rural Lowlands are predominantly Protestant in tradition, but other religious groups in rural Scotland are not likely to speak differently from anyone else by virtue of their religion. And again, if we take in the urban dialects, then there will certainly be plenty Roman Catholic – and indeed Muslim - speakers of urban Scots.

Language activists present a similarly complex political profile. The fact that I am a Gaelic learner does not mark me out as a nationalist, though I am. Brian Wilson, perhaps the most fanatically unionist minister in Labour's UK Government, is an enthusiastic Gaelic learner. There is certainly nothing to compare with, say, some of the politicised Irish learning communities of Belfast.

It is also worth pointing out, that, unlike in the Republic, or even perhaps in the North, there is very, very little tradition of learning Gaelic in Scotland. Of the 60,000 or so speakers of Gaelic in Scotland, I would doubt if more than 10,000 are learners, and of these the majority will have been largely self-taught. There has until very recently been very limited opportunity for children or adults to learn Gaelic to anything like fluency.

Scots, it is fair to say, has been much more obviously linked with nationalism. That is not to say that the SNP has favoured Scots over Gaelic - if anything, it has devoted more policy commitments to Gaelic.

Whereas for some enthusiasts of Ulster Scots there may be a potential political difficulty in that many of the older Ulster Scots poets were United Irishmen, Irish nationalists, the Scots language enthusiast in Scotland is not likely to encounter similar problems. Just about every serious Scots poet from Ramsay, and Burns onwards is a nationalist, with or without a capital N!

In an age, when Scots is seeking public funding from the Scottish Executive – and remember that our Executive is not a power sharing Executive as would be understood in Northern Ireland, but rather a coalition of two unionist parties – the nationalist associations of the Scots language movement probably do it no favours.

However, the re-establishment of the Scottish Parliament has certainly provided opportunities to debate language policy of a kind which simply did not exist a year and a half ago.

MSPs may use either of the languages, if they give notice or provide their own translation to the official reporters. The Parliament's standing orders have been amended so that motions in Scots as well as Gaelic are acceptable, and, major signage in the building is in English and Gaelic, though not Scots.

In March, there was a full debate in Gaelic – the first such debate in the Scottish Parliament since – wait for it - 1309. Only half a dozen or so members were able to contribute in Gaelic itself, but the rest took part by means of simultaneous translation into English.

The MSP I work for, Michael Russell, has tabled legislative amendments which sought to strengthen the rights of parents to have their children educated in

Gaelic. It was voted down by the Executive, who provided the chamber with the spectacle of the Minister for Gaelic arguing against increasing spending on Gaelic education to the irresponsible heights of 0.5% of the education budget.

Michael Russell has also put down numerous amendments, including ones on Gaelic signage in national parks, as well as questions seeking to establish the Executive's policy for tackling the decline in the number of Gaelic speakers.

Another question from Michael Russell recently elicited the information that the Executive have no plans in the foreseeable future to implement their manifesto pledge to introduce a Gaelic language Bill to provide secure status for the language. This measure, which is the policy of the SNP, Labour and the Liberal Democrats would have provided the right to use Gaelic in courts of law, to use Gaelic names and an increased right to Gaelic medium education.

As the Executive are not prepared to move this Bill, Michael Russell announced in August 2000 that he will move it for them. The seconder of Russell's member's Bill – which will now have to be written without the assistance of ministers or the civil service - is a Liberal Democrat, a native Gaelic speaker. I would genuinely hope that the bill will attract the cross party support which it needs. If this bill is successful, it will certainly be the most significant piece of legislation ever to promote Scottish Gaelic.

There has also been considerable discussion in the Parliament of the Scots language. Again Michael Russell recently tabled a parliamentary question asking how much money the Scottish Executive could identify as being spent on the promotion of Scots.

The answer came back that the sum total of identifiable spending on Scots is £112,500 a year. Given that early evidence is that Scots may have well over a million self-identifying speakers, this must be poorer than the public support given to just about any indigenous minority language in Europe.

For many years now, language activists and academics have been lobbying for a question on the Scots language in the 2001 Census. The case was in fact supported in principle by parliamentary committees.

If I sound bitterly partisan on this subject, it is because, though there were individual expressions of support from other members, when it came to the vote, only the SNP members, a Green and a Scottish Socialist Party member, would back this measure.

Behind the scenes for the last year, I have been pushing for measures which would give Scots better recognition, and I have to say that, by far and away, the most common brick wall that I hit is the argument that, without a standard written form, it is difficult to see how much can be given by way of official status.

The point made in my PhD with a relentless repetition, which I know irritates some Scots activists, is that, sooner or later, Scots will have to resolve that credibility problem and get itself a standard written form if it is to be taken seriously by politicians and civil servants

In conclusion, Scots and Gaelic could certainly never have achieved the public airing which they recently have had, had it not been for the Scottish Parliament. The Scottish Executive is a different matter.

As I said, everything I say is political. Objectivity is much over rated. I have to observe that practically every single measure which has been proposed in Parliament relating to Scotland's two indigenous minority languages has been voted down by the Executive party whips.

I don't think this is because of any ideological opposition to Gaelic – though I think there may well be some to Scots. Rather, I suspect it has more to do with civil service inertia and the reluctance of governments to adopt ideas which are not their own.

Another complication is that the Scottish Parliament is by no means in control over all minority language issues. Broadcasting for instance, is a "reserved power" on which, for the moment, only Westminster can legislate.

Meanwhile, Gaelic is now in a very precarious position; it will certainly die out as a community language in my lifetime, unless something radical is done now.

Scots continues to be threatened with dilution and assimilation with Scottish Standard English, and suffers from immense public and official ignorance and social prejudice.

What can be said however, is that at least now we are starting to take our minority languages seriously and they are starting to appear somewhere in Scotland's political agenda.

Language, as I said, is not politicised in the way it is in Northern Ireland. That may well prove to be a good thing for them, ensuring they have as broad an appeal as possible. On the other hand, it could be that the very intensely political status of Irish and Ulster Scots is what has ensured public funding for them through the Good Friday Agreement.

Ach, co dhiubh, gheibh sinn a mach. Tha mi dòchasach gum bidh cothrom math againn ann an Comhairle nan Eilean, a bhith a dèanamh cìnnteach gum bidh a' Ghàidhlig agus Albais a fàs ann an Alba is ann an Eirinn anns an linn ùr politigeach againn.

Oniewey, We'll fin oot. Whitiver, A hope we'll hae a chance i the cooncil o the Isles for ti mak shuir at Gaelic an Scots, growes in Ireland an i Scotland i this, oor new poleitical era thegither.

Mair As A Sheuch Atween Scotland an Ulster: Twa Policie For The Scots Leid?

Dauvit Horsbroch

Chynges in the Warld o Scots

In Aprile 1997, no lang afore the general election, the Leibral Democrat candidate for Stirlin wrate tae Rod Lovie o the *Scots Leid Associe* in Aiberdeen, an made the follaein important pynt:

> ...that the lowland Scots language has repeatedly suffered (not least within the broadcast media) from the perception that so long as Gaelic language issues are addressed then nothing more is required.[1]

At the stairt o the 1990s, it wes aye necessar tae airgue that Scots wes a leid at aw, an no juist a common patter wantin onie historie. Onlyke the Gaelic leid, Scots haesna haen the same 'romantic' link wi Celticness that whyles maks Gaelic faurben wi fowk in Scotland; the deceision makars affen hae Gaelic in mynd anent maiters o cultur/identitie, but Scots haes tae fecht tae 'get a shout'. An this is whit the Leibral Democrat wes speakin aboot; fowk in Scotland forgot that thair kintra is as muckle Germanic as it is Celtic. An A think it suits commentators in Inglan tae pit Scots, Welsh an Earse fowk awthegither as the sae-cawed "Celtic Fringe" sae we'r on the mairches o historie an politics in a British context. Whan the fowk in pouer dae think on Scots, it affen brings the creinge weil tae the fore. For in Scotland, cless abuin awthin is the quaistion that affects whit leid a bodie speaks. Naitional identitie - sib tae langage - haes taen on mair importance in the 1990s. Pairt o the problem for Scots wes aye the sair laik o onie infurmation aboot the leid, aboot its historie an reinge o uisses, an the fact that onie fowk that taen an intress in the leid aye sut aroun speakin in Inglis aboot the auld farrant Scots poyems they haed wrutten.

Houanever, it wad be richt tae say that the warld o Scots is nou the better for the puckle chynges that haes taen place, baith in cultur, an in politics. Fae aboot 1995 the govrenment in Embro, an cooncils roun aw the pairts, haes gotten uised tae fowk screivin in Scots tae thaim, an whyles a bodie even gets a bit Scots back.[2] It wes pairtlie the daeins o Gaelic steerers that set the heather ableeze at this tyme, an ordnar, no-academic fowk, gat thegither an set up thair ain groups

---

[1]   Alistair G Tough, Leibral Democrat candidate for Stirlin tae Rod Lovie, preses o the Aiberdeen Univairsitie Scots Leid Quorum, 2 Aprile, 1997. Maist o the letters quotit in this paper belang tae the papers o the Aiberdeen Univairsitie Scots Leid Quorum. It is the ettle o the AUSLQ tae deposit thir papers in the airchive o the univairsitie.

[2]   See for ensample, the letter fae Mr I Mate o the GRO (Scotland) tae Steve Murdoch, 23 Julie, 1997 (C01/k/03/30).

awthegither
for?
aye

for Scots. The general norie thay hae is this: for Scots tae win ower, tae stop the leid dwynin awa ever mair unner the owerance o Inglis, than Scots maun hae *syn* political richts an public staunin again. Steerers on behauf o Scots howped that a chynge o govrenment wad gie the fortunes o the leid a heize, an war aw for the referendum in September 1997 that socht a vote for the re-founin o the Scots pairlament. The war a lyke belief in Ulster that a Norlan Ireland Assemlie wad cast Scots alang tae.

Sae whit haes chynged in the warld o Scots in the last three year? For the first tyme, in the hairst o 1997, a meinister tuik tae dae wi Scots. Efter steerers gat on tae the new Labour govrenment, thay war tellt that "Scots falls within the ministerial remit" o Sam Galbraith, meinister for Health an the Airts.[3] At the ae tyme the Office o Scotland pit oot the first leaflet in Scots - unner the name o the govrenment - anent the referendum for the Scots pairlament. This wesna wrutten bi the govrenment, but sent tae thaim efter Scots supporters fund oot that it cuid be haen in ilka leid except Scots.[4] In Februar 1999, the Executive gree'd tae pit oot anither Scots version o hits leaflet aboot elections tae the Scots pairlament.[5] Sae twyce nou we'v haen Scots versions o govrenment blads. But it isna govrenment policie tae dae this - yet.

A doot the Scots pairlament haes made a *bittie* differ tae the staunin o the leid. Forby the twa leaflets, the Consulatative Steerin Comatee tae the pairlament gree'd that Scots shuid be recognised alang wi Gaelic. This is whit thay haed tae say in December 1998:

> We considered the use of Gaelic, Scots and other non-English languages in the Scottish Parliament, and recognised the strong historical and cultural arguments for facilitating the use of Gaelic and Scots in the Parliament.[6]

Sae Scots nou haes a place that it didna hae in the Westminster pairlament. Fae early on thay alloued for commissioners makin speeches in Scots, tho it wesna kent whither thir wad be set doun in the sederunt buiks in Scots; tho A think nou thay will. It wes decidit that a bodie wantin tae mak a Scots speech wad be weil-avisit tae gie in a version in Inglis afore haun. At a gaitherin o the procedures comatee, hauden in November 1999, it wes gree'd that the aith o allegience cuid be taen in Scots, an the fact that it haedna been in uiss at the openein o the pairlament wes an owersicht.[7] Whan a commisioner tried tae pit in an owerture in baith Inglis an Scots, she wes tellt it wesna leisome, an this led tae a wee bit

---

[3] Letter fae G Blair o the *Education and Industry* depairtment in the Office o Scotland tae the AUSLQ, 22 Julie, 1997 (OR 3355).

[4] See *Scotland's Parliament Your Choice/ The Pairliament o Scotlan Your Say*, August 1997.

[5] See *Have Your Say in May/Mak Yer Merk in Mey*, Februar 1999.

[6] *Shaping Scotland's Parliament: Report of the Consultative Steering Group on the Scottish Parliament*, Scottish Office (HMSO,Edinburgh, 1998), p.50

[7] The Procedures Comatee o the Scots pairlament as reportit in the buiks o sederunt, item 2: *The Scots Language*, 16 November, 1999.

stoushie.[8] At the stairt o 2000 this wes concedit; Scots owertures is alloued sae lang as thay hae an Inglis version alang wi thaim.[9]

Sae a bodie can tak the aith in Scots, mak a speech in Scots, an pit forrit an owerture in Scots. Anent the political pairties thairsels, the Scots Naitional Pairtie alane haes a policie on Scots, tho the ithers sic as the Leibrals an Labour haes a reference tae Scots yirdit unner thair general ettles in eddication. The SNP policie wes approven in 1996 an says:

> The SNP calls for promotion of the Scots language among adults and children, through a sufficiently-funded programme of measures planned to ensure the survival and development of the language.[10]

The SNP haes proven its commitment maist recentlie tae Scots whan the commissioners in the Scots pairlament votit in favour o Scots in the census. But the ae problem wi the SNP policie is that it is airtit at a free-staunin Scotland, an onless the ither pairties comes up wi Scots policies thairsels, the leid is aye in danger o bein taen for anither SNP ploy.

The Compare Wi Ulster

Afore 1990, ye wad a haen a sair fecht tae fin Scots fowk that thocht o Ulster Scots at aw. No monie thocht aboot thair ain leid, lat alane anither furm some ither gait. As wi the leid as a hail, fowk hiv speirt, *whit is Ulster Scots?* The poseition in Scotland, as faur as A unnerstaun it, is that in speakin o Ulster Scots we ar describin the Scots leid *in* Ulster an no a sindert leid aw its lane. Nou A ken that a hantle fowk in Ulster micht no see it juist this wey, an A can unnerstaun this fairlie. A think that Scots in Ulster haes haed tae 'bum its chat', sae tae speak, for tae staun aqual wi baith Earse an Inglis. Sae it wad be fair tae say the common norie is that we hae the ae Scots leid, striddlin the sheuch an wi features kenspeckle tae ane side or anither, but maistlie the same. The rael differ atween the twa sets o steerers is the freedom that Ulster haes tae bigg up the leid on hits syde.

The Scots speaker in Ulster buckles his belt his ain gait an haes the scowth tae dae it. Becis sae monie fowk in Scotlan speak the leid ilka day - the feck o thaim no even thinkin aboot it - it's no affa easy tae fouter aboot an experiment wi it. In ther wurds, ye'll no get awa wi muckle. But in Ulster, whaur the'r no monie speakers, an whaur the leitratur is, we can airgue, less, a bodie can get awa wi mair in the wey o langage plannin. The first political pairtie tae set furth its manifesto in Scots wesna onie in Scotland, but the DUP in Ulster. In Aprile 1997

---

[8]   The staunin Orders comatee tellt thaim that aw owertures haed tae be in Inglis sae ane anent Scots in the census in November 1999 haed tae be putten forrit in Inglis alane.

[9]   On 29t Februar, 2000 the Inglis/Scots owerture bi SNP commissioner Irene McGugan wes acceptit. Leuk tae report bi *Scots Tung Wittins*, Nu 76, Mairch 2000.

[10] Scots Naitional Pairtie *Policy: Scots language*, Juin 1996.

thay set furth *Democracie - Wi'oot Nae Dublin Owerance*. In this the pairtie intimatit

> Ulster folks haes a muckle clood hingin abune us aa, like we hinnae seen afore. The British an Dublin Governmints haes cum thegither tae mak a Yin-cleekit Airlann agin the hairt-set o the Ulster British folk.[11]

As an ootrel tae Ulster politics, it leuks tae me, fae Scotland, lyke Scots haes been taen up as pairt o the identitie o Protestant Ulster Unionism tae marra Earse Gaelic as the meisur o Catholic Ulster Naitionalism. Whan we mak compare atween Scotland an Ulster the fowk in the twa kintras wad seem tae conter ane-anither whan airguin the identitie o Scots. On the ane haun, Scots haes been taen up in Scotland bi the SNP, that wants a free-staunin Scotland, an whaur the leid is regairdit as a merk o differ wi the lave o the UK. On the ither haun, in Ulster, Scots wad seem tae be regairdit as yokin Unionists tae a British identitie in common wi Scotland. In baith cases A jalouse the Suddron - an the Welsh - wadna see it thon wey ava.

At the dowp o 1997 a report wes sent tae Tony Worthington - the meinister wi the remit for langage - bi a ceivil servan at the Office for Norlan Ireland. This debatit whither or no Ulster Scots shuid be recognised in the European Chairter for Leids o the Curn, an brocht up the hail maiter o the relationship wi Scotland. The report taen tent tae the growthe o intress in Scots in Ulster an yokit this tae whit wes takin place ower the sheuch. It fleitched the Office get thegither wi its marra in Scotland as tho thay didna juist ken whit tae dae aboot Ulster Scots.[12] Aw the same, it daes shaw that the politics o Norlan Ireland is, in pairt, haein an affect on langage policie in Scotlan, whither we lyke it or no. Bi the stairt o 1998 the fowk in Embro haed gree'd tae recognise Scots in Scotland an war tae say efter:

> The Council of Europe Charter for Regional or Minority Languages requires Member States which sign the Charter to be supportive of all their indigenous regional or minority languages. The key question is whether Scots should be recognised as a language, rather than a dialect. In specifying that Scots would be subject to Part II, the Government was recognising Scots as a language rather than a dialect.[13]

---

[11] *Democracie - Wi-oot Nae Dublin Owerance. Airts an Roadins o the Folk-Owerance Pairtie o the Ulster-British Cleek (DUP)* 1997.

[12] Cooncillor Nelson McCausland (Bilfaust); *News Release - Leaked NIO Memo on Irish Language*, 22 Aprile, 1998.

[13] C Lobban, *Constitution Group*, the Office o Scotland, tae D Horsbroch 30 Mairch, 1999 (CIB/13/6).

The UK govrenment recognised Scots throu Embro, an, becis o the kittlie talks gauin on in Ulster, cuidna dae onie less for Ulster Scots. The Guid Fryday Greement declares

> All participants recognise the importance of respect, understanding and tolerance in relation to linguistic diversity, including in Northern Ireland, the Irish language, Ulster-Scots and the languages of the various ethnic communities... [14]

Sae faur as the European Chairter an govrenment recognition raxes, Scots is traetit the exack same wey in baith Scotland an Ulster. But this gaes the same for Scots sib tae Earse an Scots Gaelic. The *Ulster Scotch Leid Societie* complenit in Aprile 1998 that whyle it walcomed the recognition o the leid in Ulster, it wesna cantie wi the wey Earse wes gien an unco heize. The *Societie* statit

> The government has made a commitment to "take resolute action to promote the Irish language" and has identified seven specific action points to implement that commitment. However, there is no corresponding commitment to take resolute action to promote the Ulster-Scots language. [15]

We can mak a direck compare wi Gaelic an Scots in Scotland. In Mairch 1999 the Office o Scotland wrate tae Scots steerers:

> Part II of the Charter requires the Member State to apply 35 pargaraphs or sub-pargarpahs in support of the specified language. We are in a position to do this for Gaelic, but we are not in respect of Scots. [16]

As faur back as 1996 the lyne comin oot o the Office o Scotland wes this : "The Government's view is that the Scots language is an element of everyday speech for many people in Scotland and that the position of the Scots language is not, therefore, as fragile as that of Gaelic." [17] In the Whyte Paper on Scotland's pairlament in 1998 Gaelic wes mintit but Scots wesna, an naether did Scots get a shout in the cultural ettles o the Labour-Leibral admeinistration in the hairst o 1999. In baith Scotland an Ulster the fowk in pouer daena seem tae be as fashed aboot Scots as thay ar wi the twa Gaelic leids.

In 1998, the *Ulster Scotch Leid Societie* cawed for the founin o an Ulster-Scots Langage Trust, an Ulster Scots Centre, an a wirkin pairtie on the leid. Memmers o the *Societie* gat thegither wi fowk in the *Scots Language Resource*

---

[14] Leuk tae *The Good Friday Agreement*.
[15] *Ulster Scotch Leid Societie*, press statement 16t Aprile, 1998.
[16] C Lobban, *Constitution Group*, tae D Horsbroch 30 Mairch, 1999.
[17] G Ingram, *Education and Industry* depairtment, Office o Scotland tae J Engebretsen 12 August 1996 (JUG/1/38).

Centre at the stairt o 1999 an pit forrit thair ploys for forderin the leid on baith sydes o the sheuch. Houanever, the parteiclar adaes in Norlan Ireland - that we cry the tribbles - mean that the leid in Ulster is taen faur mair serious bi the heich heid anes nor it is in Scotland. For this reason, Ulster Scots micht weil lowp forrit in the near oncome an pit in the shadda the sma gains made bi speakers in Scotland. This is patent tae fowk anent the maiter o siller.

A wad airgue that Scots in Ulster is better tochert nor it is in Scotland as an affcome o the Guid Fryday Greement. Scots fowk war fell surprised bi news in the hairst o 1999 that Scots in Ulster wad aiblins get a million poun or mair fae baith the govrenments o Dublin an the Unitit Kinrik. Scots conseidered aw the haurd campainin an the fact that thay cuidna even get Scots in the Census, lat alane onie siller.

Unner pairt 23 o the Naitional Heritage (Scotland) Act o 1985, the Office o Scotland can gie siller tae groups forderin Scots; the first peyments war made in the year 1990-91. In this year Scots wes gien £15,000 bi the govrenment. Slawlie ower the 1990s this feigur gaed up an doun, an wes as muckle as £130,000 at ae pynt, but never onie mair. Maist o this siller wes gien tae the SNDA or DOST an a wee tait tae the *Scots Language Resource Centre* in Perth. The General Register Office for Scotland, efter speirin roun the kintra in 1996, cam oot wi an official reckonin o 1.5 million speakers or 30% o fowk in Scotland. We can mak compare wi baith Scots Gaelic an Ulster Scots.[18]

Gauin bi the wabsteid o the Executive o Scotland, parteiclar fundin for Gaelic stairtit in 1979 at juist £100,000. Bi 2002, this wull be heized tae £12,678,000, comprehendin siller for eddication, braidcastin an airts projecks. The nummer o speakers at the 1991 census wes 69,510 or 1.4% o fowk in Scotland.[19]

In the years 1998-99 Scots in Ulster gat £101,000 fundin - marra wi the leid in Scotland - an the *Ulster Scotch Leid Societie* reckons aboot 100,000 speakers in the province. Unner the Guid Fryday Greement the Earse an UK govrenments gree'd tae set up jynt bodies athort the border that wad comprehend Earse Gaelic an Ulster Scots. The bodie wirkin for Scots wad be steidit in Donegal an the ane for Earse in Bilfaust. Earse Gaelic wad be peyed up tae £12 million wi 25% comin fae the UK whyle Ulster Scots wad get £1 million wi the UK gien £750,000.[20] A gaither that this feigur micht nou be even mair. This wad mean that even the Dublin govrenment wad be gien mair tae Scots in Ulster nor the admeinistration haes ever gien tae the leid in its hame kintra.

Tae say that Scots speakers in Scotland is clean scunnert isna sayin it aw. The'r no scunnert wi Gaelic or Ulster Scots, but wi thair ain govrenment for no haein a wycelike policie, an for haein twa-staunarts in whit is meant tae be the ae state. *Scots Tung*, a Scots group in Musselburgh, haed this comment tae mak in thair *Wittins*:

---

[18] For feigurs on thir leuk tae Executive o Scotland wabsteid *Scots Language Factsheet*.

[19] Office o Scotland, *Education and Industry* depairtment, *Gaelic in Scotland Factsheet*, Aprile 1999.

[20] Taen fae ootlyne report bi Tom Band *Scots Leid Associe* representative at gaitherin o depute comatee o EBLUL 1 September, 1999.

It's aye guid tae see a wee bairn weel fendit for, but whit kinna fowk
wad juist gaun by an leave its mither tae sterve? [21]

Whit Wey No Muckle Support in Scotland?

Tho the admeinistration in Scotland haes recognised Scots, it haes aye harled it s ?
feet ower gien active support. Donald Dewar haes lat on a puckle tyme that he is
sweirt tae gie the kin o support tae Scots that the Executive o Scotland nou gies
tae Gaelic. Pairt o the problem for Scots in Scotland is that sae monie supporters
oxter alang wi the SNP. On ane haun SNP fowk feel that the Unionist pairties is
feart for Scots, faur mair nor Gaelic. Efter aw, wi sae monie fowk speakin Scots -
or kennin a guid bit o it - an seein it as pairt an paircel o thair naitional identitie, it
cuid be mair o a problem nor Gaelic tae the British state. On the subjeck o the
census the SNP memmer at Westminster for Gallowa sayed in 1998:

> I have always thought it unlikely that a fundamentally Anglo-centric
> administration like this Labour government would be sympathetic to
> the reasons why Scots should be on the census. The correspondence
> that I have had with ministers on this issue has certainly not convinced
> me otherwise.[22]

Mair recentlie a Torie in the Scots pairlament described support for Scots as "
almost to the point of political correctness" and that it wad " only serve to expose
the Parliament to further ridicule that would be wise to avoid."[23] Voters micht
conseider that the pairties is daein a guid eneuch job in makin a gowk o the
pairlament thairsels, athoot hein Scots haein onie pairt o it. Ploys tae mak uiss o Scots
in the wee scuil in the coontie o Angus war described as "narrow nationalism" bi
a Torie cooncillor in Juin 1999,[24] an naethin cuid be mair revealin o attitudes nor
the vote anent Scots in the census that taen place in Februar; aw the Unionist
pairties votit agin it, but aw the pairties wantin a free-staunin Scotland votit for
it.[25] It's patent nou, A think, that Scots is seen as a naitionalist quaistion in
Scotland an this is whit wey the admeinstration hums an haws ower giein it onie
heize.

---

[21] *Scots Tung Wittins*, Nu 73 December, 1999.

[22] Letter fae A Morgan commissioner at Westminster for Gallowa an Upper Nithsdale tae
AUSLQ 15 Mey, 1998 (GPM/AM).

[23] B Monteith, commissioner tae the Scots pairlament for Mid Scotland an Fife at
gaitherin o the Procedures comatee, 16 November, 1999.

[24] Reportit in *The Scotsman*, I Juin 1999.

[25] The buiks o sederunt o the Scots pairlament reportit on page 1124 that the vote taen on
16t Februar, 2000 gaed as follaes: for 28 SNP, 1 Green, 1 Independent Labour, 1 Scots
socialist pairtie (awthegither 31); agin 49 Labour, 15 Torie, 11 Leibral Democrat
(awthegither 75); bydin awa 1 Leebral Democrat.

On baith sydes o the sheuch fowk haes been reared in the scuils an in public life tae creinge whan the leid is uised. The adverteisment for the Unner Editor o Inglis an Ulster Scots - for the Assemlie - brocht furth the ordnar comments. The *Irish News* prentit a cairtoon shawin ane cheil speakin an anither speirin whither he wes pittin in for the job or haed juist swallied his wallies.[26] But the same can be sayed for Gaelic; ane screiver in the *Scottish Sun* cryed Gaelic speakers "porridge guzzlers" no lang syne. Sic tuim-heidit views on the richts o leids is common in baith the UK an Ireland. In Scotland itsel we affen get cauld kail fae the meidia; *The Herald* paper commentit in December 1997 " It would be of no help if Scots were to receive the kind of artificial boost which, with EU funding, has given Gaelic an unnatural prominence which might in the longer term prove unhealthy."[27] Monie Scots speakers feel that staunart Inglis - bein the leid o nane but a curn in govrenment - is the leid that is gien the 'artificial boost' in public lyfe.

Ane ither thing that daesna help Scots muckle is the wey fowk affen pickle the leid lyke ferlies in jaurs tae be putten awa in museums. It is sicna fowk that get maist o the scant siller for Scots in Scotland, but a speech communitie haes mair wants nor thon alane. Bi no takin tent tae the ither wants, we hiv gien the idea that govrenment juist haes tae rax a bit bawbees intae dictionar projecks an Scots is sairtit. We'r in danger o the siller no streitchin tae the leivin leid.

The Ae Douce Police for Scots?

Afore Scots can mak forrit on baith sydes o the sheuch A wad say faur mair fowk wants tae courrie-up wi ane anither, an stairt speakin. The'r a danger that gin we daena caw cannie wi this leid, than we ar awa tae get twa policie that wull shed it ance an for aw. Anent the wrutten leid, we want tae come tae faur mair accord on general uiss. Readin Scots wrutten in Ulster tae Scots wrutten in Scotland, it leuks lyke the'r faur mair o an ettle tae mak Ulster Scots leuk as different fae Inglis as can be. Nane o us is athoot sin whan it comes tae this. Whither we'r steerin for Earse, Welsh, Scots Gaelic or Scots - an whyles even Inglis itsel - we aw fouter aboot wi the leids thinkin tae mak thaim shouder the burden o modren life. We ar sweirt tae uise guid Latinate wurds becis we hiv been led tae think o thaim as belangin tae Inglis alane, sae we darg awa on lang-nebbit weys o sayin things. A ken, A'v been doun this gait; whyles ye pull it aff, but whyles ye can mak a richt bourach o yer bit screive, whither ye'r versant or learner. Scots daes hae a howe caudron o vocabular that screivers an ithers can deek intil athoot haein tae mak up new anes. A wad fleitch steerers in Ulster doun this gait gin thay arna wantin tae fleg fowk.

Gin Scots speakers on baith sydes o the sheuch cuid come thegither mair affen, trate Scots as the ae leid, an caw cannie wi the leitratur we set furth, A

---

[26] Cairtoon bi I Knox in *Irish News* (Bilfaust), 10 Februar 1999.
[27] Leader Comment, *The Herald*, 19 December, 1997.

daena think we can gae faur wrang. An it wadna dae us onie hairm tae forgaither wi a Gaelic speaker ance in a whylie aether.

Boundaries, Diversity and Inter-culturalism: The Case of Ulster Scots

Mark Adair

Talking and thinking across boundaries

Community relations work is about many things. In its cultural aspect, however, it seeks to encourage a reconciled diversity between the traditions and experiences of local communities. It acknowledges the importance of cultural and political differences, but also the need for these to be better managed and understood. It emphasises the benefits of dialogue and the ill effects of division. It also works to explore how we might celebrate our diverse cultures and traditions without unravelling society into what Arthur Schlesinger has called "a quarrelsome spatter of enclaves, ghettos and tribes".[1] Community relations insists that if we are to rub along, rather than rub each other out, then all of us have responsibilities and promises to keep.

A society filled with differences is teeming with provocation. Whether we cause or take offence, however, is a matter of choice. Either way, our actions have consequences. Our shared task in this new century will be to find ways of giving space and respect to each other. The alternative is a form of identity politics which exaggerates differences, turns culture into a series of competing caricatures, and makes further separations almost inevitable.

The challenge facing Northern Ireland is one which confronts pluralist societies throughout these islands and the world. Talking and thinking across boundaries is the antidote everywhere prescribed. It's the pragmatic and only sensible response to diversity. Creating a socially inclusive and cohesive society from out of all of this difference requires that we have both the language and experience of community, but also a second/shared language of citizenship which extends beyond and connects our different communities and ethnicities. Both are necessary. Community relations work seeks to encourage their combined adoption by local communities.

Our relations with others are made easier if we recognise that no culture is hermetically sealed; that all cultures influence and are influenced by others and that none of our traditions are changeless, invariant or static. As a recent UNESCO report observes, "all cultures are in a state of constant flux, driven by internal and external factors".[2] Cultures, unlike clocks, cannot be stopped nor indeed can their boundaries be clearly set. Our world in Louis MacNeice's phrase is "suddener and more of it than we think".[3]

No shame in being various

Northern Ireland has been described as "a shared region of these islands", a place where "Ireland and Britain permeate one another",[4] albeit not always to good harmonious effect. The interplay of these diverse traditions and experiences, however, has been the feature of life here over several hundred years. Our pasts are inextricably linked. Cross channel and cultural borrowings have made us who we are. There is nothing unmixed about the people or traditions of Ulster. Whilst politics and religion may emphasise separation, cultural influences have overspilled boundaries. Apparently distinctive traditions have changed through dialogue and encounter with others. Cultural influences from Britain, Ireland and elsewhere have intermingled to create a diversity which can only be partly understood in terms of political categories. Our cultural traditions cannot easily be collapsed into the simple stories of Ireland's competing nationalisms. Common sense and the historical record insists that it shouldn't be done.

We do damage to our self-understanding and relations with others, by writing people and complexity out of the past. History is full of ambivalences, confusions and borrowings. In this respect it's as jumbled and as various as our own lives. In attempting to make sense of it, we shouldn't ignore uncomfortable realities or differences. There is no straight line connecting the past and present realities. History, like culture, runs zigzag. Properly read, it should, and does, raise as many difficult questions as it offers easy answers.

Whilst the borders between our cultural and political experiences are real, they have also to some degree been permeable. Informed cultural debate should acknowledge this overlap. The idea of pure communities is a fiction best grown out of. We are all mongrels now and would benefit from acknowledging this diverse inheritance. There's no shame in being various.

Identity with an ugly face

Societies, it is said are strong to the extent that they can accommodate differences without actually falling apart. Diversity, in other words, offers potential benefits for everyone. That's the theory. It requires flexibility and common sense, however, to make it work. In a place more recently accustomed to cultural defence rather than negotiation, this can be difficult to achieve. Our diversity has too often been reduced to a form of cultural assertion, the effect of which, whether intentional or otherwise, has been to threaten and exclude. Culture with an ugly face has turned differences into division, tested neighbourliness to its limits and allowed one form of identity politics to create its opposite.

Doing our own thing regardless of the consequences is a turning away from the possibilities of a shared society. It builds walls rather than bridges and creates ghettos in the name of self-esteem. Diversity without respect for others can do much to make a bad situation worse. Very often that's the intention of those involved. It can work to our mutual advantage, however, if based on a recognition that our lives and communities are enriched through dialogue with others. Pluralism has much to recommend it. As Robert Hughes observes "in society, as in farming, monoculture works poorly. It exhausts the soil".[5] Much better to take our chances with inter-culturalism, than to rely on the meagre (and predictable) harvest of going it alone.

A properly functioning society will be one which recognises the complex and overlapping histories of local communities and which acknowledges the links which connect our region to Britain, Ireland and the World. Influences from all points of the compass have converged on this place and none should be denied.

History's changing dress code

All historical periods are times of transition, for change is a characteristic of them all. The speed and scale of social and other transformations in our own time, however, has been disconcerting for many of us. In this uncertain environment, cultural traditions can seem to offer connections to a more settled past. Reclaiming the songs, music-making and language of our forbears has many benefits, not least as a balm for the insecurities of the present. Such activities are important and can also assist us in taking a longer view of cultural and historical developments. Over-indulgence in memory, however, may also serve to shut out present experience and lead to the assumption that our communities and cultures are fixed: that a full-stop was reached some time ago in their respective development. This would be unfortunate. Yesterday's achievements may be interesting and worthwhile, but these shouldn't be allowed to embargo current or future possibilities. Cultures and communities are living things, forever in the making. Whilst we cannot function without a recognisable past, we are paralysed unless we seek to change and enlarge upon it.

The Ulster-Scots experience is still unfolding as it absorbs experiences/influences unimagined by previous generations. The relevance of Scotland, Ulster and different cultural practices to our self-identity has changed overtime and will continue to do so. If the work of the Heritage Council is to be more than mere nostalgism, therefore, it must engage with this dynamic and its open-ended potential. History never ends, it just changes its dress code. Similarly, whilst cultures may be influenced by the past, their continued relevance and usefulness depends on constant interaction with the present. Living traditions combine old and new in ever changing patterns. They are as fluid and as diverse as the people whose lives they reflect.

More than an insular fable

Ulster-Scots need not be an insular fable. It should acknowledge that Protestants and Catholics have been part of this experience, and that cross-channel connections are not necessarily a shorthand term for unionism. Acknowledgement should also be given to how Irish life, in all its different aspects, has impacted on the peoples of this place. Wider British, European and other influences have also shaped an historical and cultural experience which has been neither singular nor constant. The interplay between communities in Scotland and the north-east of Ireland has been complex and various. Traditions and identities have ebbed and flowed throughout the contemporary period. All are necessary to a full understanding of how the geographical closeness of these islands has impacted on our politics, religion and culture. Recovering, and making sense of these many encounters may well suggest an inter-dependence which extends beyond politics.

Ulster-Scots activities must be inclusive in their engagement with past and present realities. Whilst culture has legitimate political uses, it would be unfortunate if the shared, albeit different, experiences which we have in our relations with Scotland, were to be narrowed into the story of this or that community. Being caught up in the interplay between our two islands has not, nor should it preclude other affiliations, loyalties or influences. The variety and adaptability of the Ulster-Scots experience should continue to be reflected in the work of the Heritage Council.

A story big enough for all of us

In some respects, all traditions and communities are invented things, stories which we create in order to understand the present and influence the future. The Irish cultural and literary revival with its selective reading of the past was one of the most successful instances of myth-making with a purpose. It was a vision which narrowed in the telling, however, and left much history and not a few people out. Cultural connections and borrowings weren't a strong feature of its analysis. Complexity was ignored in favour of more simple truths. As a feel-good exercise in new definitions of Irishness, it was a project which had serious limitations, not least for unionists' sense of belonging. The lesson for Ulster-Scots enthusiasts is clear. In documenting and celebrating our Scottish connections, we should do nothing to obscure the inclusive nature of this inheritance. Ulster-Scots needn't and shouldn't get caught up in some zero sum game of opposing cultural certainties. It is a story big and inclusive enough for all of us.

As one commentator has observed, "when a single beam is mistaken for the sun, all other rays are extinguished".[6] Let's not make that mistake. Here's to a shared and diverse future in which we have the confidence to let the whole sun shine in.

Notes

1   Arthur M. Schlesinger, Jnr. *The Disuniting of America: Reflections on a Multi-Cultural Society.* (New York: Simon and Schuster, 1998) p. 147

2   UNESCO Report: *Cultural Heritage and Language.* p. 34

3   Louis MacNiece. 'Snow'. In *The Collected Poems of Louis MacNiece.* edited by E.R. Dodds (London: Faber and Faber, 1979) p. 34

4   Edna Longley, *From Kathleen to Anorexia: The Breakdown of Irelands.* (Attic Press, 1990) p. 24

5   Robert Hughes. *The Culture of Complaint.* (Oxford: Oxford Univesity Press, 1993) p. 14

6   Francis Pym. *The Politics of Consent.* (London: Hamish Hamilton, 1984) p. 193